KEEPING

AN
ALLOTMENT

KEEPING

AN
ALLOTMENT

GROWING YOUR
OWN FRUIT AND
VEGETABLES

Kevin Forbes

AURA

This edition published in 2010
by Baker & Taylor (UK) Limited,
Bicester, Oxfordshire

Copyright © 2010 Arcturus Publishing Limited
26/27 Bickels Yard, 151–153 Bermondsey Street
London SE1 3HA

ISBN: 978-1-90723-103-2
AD001475EN

Printed in China

CONTENTS

INTRODUCTION

Imagine escaping the hustle and bustle of everyday life and finding an oasis of tranquility just around the corner from your home. Growing fruit, vegetables and flowers on an allotment is not only a fantastic way of giving wildlife a place to live and feed, but it will also keep you fit.

Keeping an allotment will take you outside to work with nature and you will literally be able to enjoy the fruits of your labour. Even if your gardening experience has thus far only stretched to keeping a few tubs in your courtyard garden or a couple of pots of herbs on your windowsill, hopefully with the help of this book and the advice of your newfound friends at the allotment site, you will find this a rewarding and beneficial challenge.

The thrill of seeing your first seeds poking their heads through the soil is a memory that will stay with you for years. Imagine how satisfying it will be when you see your whole plot turned into a fertile site full of your favourite fruit and vegetables. Allotment gardening is a fantastic opportunity to grow the sort of food you love without spending a fortune. You will never need to spend money again on those over-priced packets of salad leaves or vine-grown tomatoes; instead you can sow a packet of seeds and all for the cost of just one bag. Potatoes, which are very easy to grow, can grace your table at every meal and you can choose exactly the variety that your family prefers. As you become more adventurous, you can even start your own asparagus bed; there is nothing quite like the taste of asparagus that has only just been cropped and cooked.

Added to the pleasures of eating your own produce you can be happy in the knowledge that it is totally fresh and completely free of any chemicals. This book aims to show you how to grow your crops organically, with the least amount of fuss and lists easy-to-grow produce that is full of flavour. At the end of the book are a few recipes to try using your seasonal fruit and vegetables.

Allotments are becoming increasingly popular as people are becoming more environmentally aware. We haven't all got enough space to grow our own produce, so more people are turning to renting a plot and learning to watch the pennies.

Getting Started

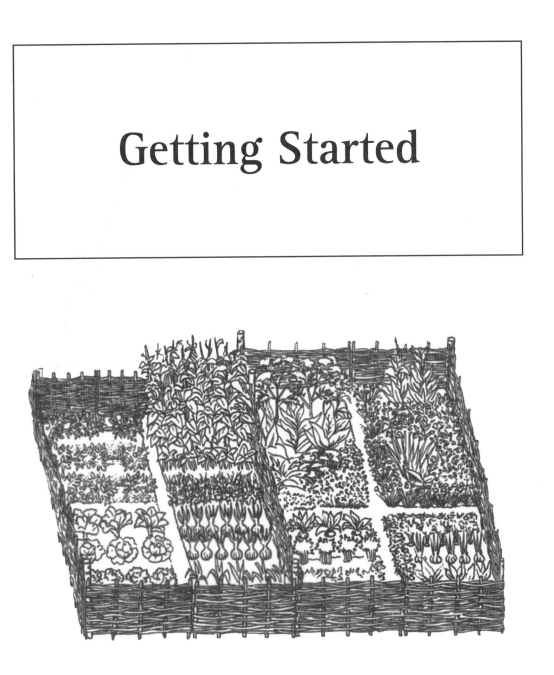

ALLOTMENTS AND LANDSHARE

In the United Kingdom, an allotment is a small parcel of land rented to individuals for the purpose of growing fruit, vegetables and other plants. There is no set size, but the average plot is around 10 square rods or 253 square metres. Renting one won't break the bank either – many local authorities only charge a small sum per year.

The benefits of growing your own food are immense. Quite apart from improving the quality of life in terms of general health, it is great fun. But in the very beginning of the history of allotments, growing vegetables was an absolute necessity. Allotments came into being in the time of the Saxons, who would clear an area of commonland to grow crops to sustain their families. After the Norman Conquest in 1066, land ownership became more concentrated and fell into the hands of manorial lords, monasteries and even the Church.

The 17th and 18th centuries saw more and more and more people moving from rural areas into the increasingly industrialized cities to find work. Conditions were not good, as overcrowding in both working and living spaces and inadequate nutrition led to poor health. This move from a subsistence economy to the more modern industrial system led to an increase in the number of poor who, without the benefits of a social security system, could literally starve for lack of food or the land on which to grow their own.

Germany was the first country to set up 'gardens for the poor', offering people the chance to get out into the open air and grow their own food. People jumped at the chance of obtaining a piece of enclosed land called a *Schrebergarten* (allotment). The idea gradually spread to other parts of Europe, with Holland and Denmark adopting the allotment movement.

The history of the British allotment can be traced back to the feudal system and the steady loss of common land from the 16th century onwards. By 1818, Acts of Parliament meant that more than five million acres of otherwise common land had been enclosed, denying those without land any means of growing their own food. To try to reduce poverty and the spread of disease, and realizing that too much common land had been commandeered, the government passed the General Enclosure Act. This meant that land became accessible to the under-privileged and also protected the interests of small proprietors. The act required that 'field gardens' of a quarter of an acre were made available to the public; this was really the start of allotments as we know them today. Although the act had good intentions, it actually failed in its purpose, because out of the 615,000 acres originally enclosed by the government, only 2,200 acres were released for the use of allotments.

Allotments soon spread into urban areas, the first ones appearing as 'guinea gardens' on the outskirts of Birmingham. These were short-lived, however, as the land was quickly requisitioned to build much needed housing.

THE ALLOTMENT ACT 1887

The Allotment Act of 1887 obliged local authorities to provide allotments if there was a demand for them. Local authorities tried to resist complying with this act and it had to be revised in 1908 with the Smallholding and Allotment Act in 1907. This act imposed responsibilities on parish, urban and borough councils to provide allotments. The Victorians were thrilled with the act, hoping that working on the land would help to prevent the 'degeneracy' of the working classes.

WARTIME

The First World War prompted a huge growth in the number of allotments. The figures escalated from 600,000 to 1,500,000, as people depended on home-grown produce. Widespread unemployment during the 1920s and 1930s kept them going and the onset of the Second World War increased the role of allotments further. Many farm workers were called to fight for their country and blockades from Germany caused food shortages, necessitating the need to grow food on every piece of available land. Allotments became a common feature in towns and cities, with the famous 'Dig for Victory' posters everywhere educating people on how to produce their own food and contribute to the war effort.

The end of the war saw quite a drastic fall in the demand for allotments, as more and more land was allocated to building sites. This led to the re-establishment of the Allotments Advisory Board, which in 1949 recommended that a provision of 4 acres should be alloted to every 1,000 head of population. This in turn led to the Allotment Act of 1950.

DECLINE AND RISE

By the 1970s there were approximately 500,000 allotment sites, which continued to decline throughout the decade. There wasn't really an upsurge in demand until the television series *The Good Life,* which ran from 1975 to 1978. The series showed a young couple who tried to become self-sufficient by converting their suburban back garden into an allotment-style smallholding; it encouraged other people to have a go, too.

By 1996, there were approximately 297,000 plots available and as concerns about genetically modified foods, chemical pollution and general contamination of our food have grown, we are seeing an increase in demand. This renewed interest has seen empty plots filled and long waiting lists for allotments that previously had high vacancy rates. Allotmenteering is timeless; you will see people of all ages and from all walks of life getting down and dirty. So why not call your local council today and get digging!

HOW MUCH TIME WILL I NEED?

This is a question that people frequently ask and it is impossible to say that an allotment will not take up a lot of your time. The spring and summer months are the most demanding and will require at least two hours twice a week and four hours at a weekend. This is the sort of commitment you will need to make. The pace is slower during the autumn and winter months, so two hours a week during this period should be sufficient. If you want to keep your plot looking tidy and free of weeds, you will need to be fairly dedicated, but you will soon find that your allotment will become a welcome escape at the end of a busy day.

The allotment is an ideal place to take children, as it is a safe enclosed place away from traffic. They will benefit from being outside and can also learn the benefits of growing vegetables for themselves. You could even encourage them by making a small pond: dig a hole and insert a plastic washing-up bowl to act as a mini pond. This should encourage wildlife and if you are lucky enough to find some frog spawn in a local pond, you can get your children to take some back and put it in their pond. By attracting frogs to your site, you will suffer less damage from slugs and alleviate the need for pesticides.

Depending on the regulations of your local council, some allotments allow you to keep small livestock – for example, chickens – but cockerels are probably not a good idea, as they could cause annoyance with their early-morning alarm calls.

If you work full time and your leisure time is limited, you might like to consider sharing an allotment with a friend. Many people give up their allotments in the first year because they realize they have taken on too much; by sharing the load you can enjoy it rather than find it becoming a chore. It is also a great way of getting together on a summer's evening, and working alongside a companion can help to make even the toughest jobs more pleasurable. Only one person can sign the allotment agreement, so if it is in your name you will need to remember that you will be the one receiving the letters if you fail to keep your allotment in tip-top condition. It is also a good idea to have some kind of financial agreement with regards to the cost of tools and produce so that everything can be equally shared out at the end of the day without one person feeling they deserve more than the other.

Some allotment societies try to encourage newcomers by offering smaller, cheaper, beginner's plots, with the option of taking more land at the end of the first year. If, however, after careful consideration you feel that an allotment would be too much work, you can still enjoy the benefits of fresh produce by making part of your garden available or by having pots and grow bags on your patio. Do not be put off completely; everyone can have a go at growing their own fruit and vegetables.

GETTING TO KNOW THE ALLOTMENT COMMUNITY

You will find a mixed assortment of people in the allotment community. Some retired, some people in full-time employment and youngsters who are eager to be as self-sufficient as possible. Then you will find those that are happy to lean on their fork handle and chat for hours or those people who want to tend their plot and leave without becoming involved with anyone else. It is up to you just how involved you want to become with the rest of the community. Don't be afraid to ask advice from someone who has a well-maintained

plot with a good variety of produce; they will probably have plenty of tips to give you. Most people will be delighted that you are taking an interest and you will soon look forward to going to your allotment and interacting with your new friends.

As a plot holder you will be invited to attend meetings either by your local allotment association or council. You might think this could be a bit boring, but remember it is a great way to meet the rest of the allotment community and learn what they expect from you with regard to maintaining your plot. You should find the dates and times of your allotment association meetings on the notice board at the allotment site.

Don't fall into the trap of becoming jealous of your neighbours' plots and judging your own crop by the size of theirs. Enjoy the experience of growing and producing your own food, rather than trying to keep up with the Jones's.

WHY ORGANIC?

Organic gardening is growing produce without the use of any artificial chemicals or pesticides; in other words, taking advantage of the natural biodiversity that surrounds us every day. Ladybirds and other beneficial insects, birds, snakes, hedgehogs etc., all play a part in keeping the balance right. It is our responsibility to maintain the natural health of the soil, keeping it well fertilized and choosing the appropriate plants to encourage wildlife. It doesn't make any sense at all to grow some perfect vegetables and then contaminate them by spraying synthetic chemicals on or near them. In that case, you might just as well go and buy the pristine examples found on supermarket shelves.

By keeping your allotment organic, you are helping to reduce your own carbon footprint. If your allotment is in a built-up urban area, you will also be contributing to an essential biodiversity and improving the atmosphere in your district.

Hopefully you are now convinced that an allotment is for you. The next sections explore how to go about acquiring your plot.

WHY SHARE LAND?

As more and more people are taking to growing their own produce, land is in great demand. As the waiting lists get longer for allotment plots, people are trying to find other places in which to grow their own fruit and vegetables. Many farmers and landowners are answering this demand by offering portions of their land for rent. This is a fairly new and exciting trend, which makes growing vegetables accessible to everyone.

The National Trust is also playing its part by creating 1,000 new allotment plots, which they hope to have available by 2013. The National Trust owns many different types of land, so the plots will not always be on their heritage sites.

A landshare website has been set up by the British chef Hugh Fearnley-Whittingstall, who is an avid campaigner for growing your own produce. This site can be found at www.landshare.net and will give you all the latest information available.

Land is becoming available throughout England, Wales and Northern Ireland, so it doesn't matter where you live. If you don't have access to an allotment or piece of land for growing, you can take advantage of the landshare system on your doorstep.

ALLOTMENTS OVERSEAS

GERMANY

Although allotments are considered to be a very British tradition, there is evidence of similar schemes overseas, one example being in Germany. Allotments or land used for growing produce was connected to the period of industrialization in Europe during the 19th century. People migrated from rural areas into the cities in search of work and a way to improve their lifestyle. Many of these people had endured serious hardships and most arrived suffering from malnutrition.

Aware of their plight, churches and local authorities put their heads together and came up with the idea of providing open spaces for the migrants to grow their own food. These were initially called 'gardens for the poor', but later acquired the name 'allotment gardens'.

The allotment scheme reached its peak shortly after 1864, when a school principal by the name of Ernst Innozenz Hauschild set up the Schreber Movement. This movement involved leasing land to encourage children to take exercise in a healthy environment. Many of these spaces included gardens, which were quickly adopted by many of the children's parents to grow their own vegetables. This type of garden became very popular, not only in Germany, but also in Austria, Sweden and Switzerland.

Just as in the UK, these allotments became of prime importance during both world wars. Nutritious food was hard to come by and any that was available on the black market was usually beyond the reach of the majority of the population due to severe shortages of cash. The production of fresh produce became paramount for the survival and health of the population.

SWEDEN

The very first allotment garden in Sweden was established in Malmö in 1895 and was the inspiration of an upper-class lady by the name of Anna Lindhagen. She had seen allotment gardens in neighbouring Copenhagen and was so impressed with the idea that she decided to write a book about them. It was her enthusiasm that encouraged the local authorities to set aside certain pieces of land for cultivation.

The Swedis Federation of Leisure Gardening was founded in 1921 and today it represents more than 26,000 allotments and leisure gardens.

THE PHILIPPINES

The allotment garden is a relatively new idea in the Philippines and did not appear until 2003. It was set up in Cagayan de Oro City, Northern Mindanao, as part of a European Union-funded project. Aided and encouraged by the German Embassy in Manila, this has grown rapidly into five self-sustaining gardens.

The scheme has been so successful in the Philippines that they are now in the process of setting up gardens within the premises of elementary schools. Gardeners who have had access to the allotments grow a variety of vegetables and tropical fruits and are allowed to keep small livestock. They have also been given permission to build fish ponds to breed fish in an effort to provide protein in their diets. Each garden has a compost heap where biodegradable waste from the garden and neighbouring households is converted into organic fertilizer. This has helped to alleviate the major problem of waste within the city areas. All the gardens are also fitted with ecological sanitation toilets.

DENMARK

When Danish architects decided to build upwards instead of outwards to save space, residents found they had little or no garden at all. Because they had nowhere to grow vegetables or flowers they complained to the local authorities, who came up with the idea of offering allotment space. Many of the urban residents who had only just moved into the cities from the country, were used to growing their own food, so they jumped at the chance of being able to rent land to cultivate their own produce.

Sunday became 'allotment' day and whole families would spend their precious leisure time tending their plots. Like many European countries, these allotments became vitally important during the war years, when food was at a premium. In 1916, the Allotment Garden Federation of Denmark was formed and it was able to offer advice and even gave trial plots to encourage people to start cultivating their own piece of land. The allotment garden movement reached its peak during the Second World War, with more than 100,000 plots available.

As the economy improved, the demand for this type of garden declined and many of these precious sites were buried under the concrete of motorways built for the growing number of cars. Any plots that survived were often too close to the roads and the produce became contaminated, meaning that many were just abandoned.

Today, however, the demand for allotments is growing in Denmark once again. To try to solve the problem of demand being greater than supply, the Ministry of Agriculture has bought up any available green spaces and is renting them out as allotments on a long-term basis.

CUBA

Before the revolution in 1959, almost half of the agricultural land in Cuba was owned by just one per cent of the people. After the revolution, agriculture was nationalized and the majority of the land was turned over to producing sugar cane. This was used as a trading commodity with the USSR in return for machinery, fuel, fertilizers and reasonably priced food. However, when the USSR collapsed in 1990, Cuba struggled to produce enough food to sustain its own people. People were literally starving to death and the government knew they needed to take radical action. The Ministry of Agriculture established an urban gardening scheme, which produced as many as 25,000 *huertos* or allotments by 1995. In addition to these, larger-scaled *organoponicos*, or market gardens, were provided in an effort to build up enough supplies of much-needed fresh produce.

Every village in Cuba was given a trained agronomist to help families get started. Children were encouraged to learn how to grow vegetables, herbs and fruit in local school gardens. They introduced organic growing methods and, in 1996, Havana passed a bylaw stating that only organic methods could be used when growing food. Today, Cuba leads the world in many aspects of organic food production, particularly in the compost made from worm farms.

ITALY AND SPAIN

The traditional allotment scheme that allows individuals to rent plots from an association or council is not really an established tradition in either Spain or Italy. There is, however, an ancient tradition of growing vegetables on small plots called *huertos*, situated outside towns and villages. These *huertos* were introduced by the Moors, who occupied Spain for more than 800 years. When Spain was recaptured by the Christians in 1492, much of the land was turned over to the monasteries, whose monks grew citrus fruit and olives. It is still possible to obtain plots of land for self-cultivation, but it is not on such a large scale as in the rest of Europe.

ACQUIRING YOUR ALLOTMENT

Having decided that you have the time and the inclination to tend an allotment, you now need to start the hunt to find a suitable plot. If you are already aware of an allotment site close to your home, then it is probably a good idea to go down there and ask some of the plot holders how to apply for a plot. You will probably find that they are only too happy to help, but if there is no one around, then you should find a notice board that can give you the name of the authority to contact. Failing that, contact your local parish, town, borough, city or district council or make enquiries at your local library.

The last few years have seen a tremendous upsurge in the number of people wanting an allotment and a whole new generation of young families are rolling up their sleeves and getting their hands dirty. Because so many plots have been lost in the past two decades to make way for development, the waiting lists in some parts of the country are exceptionally long. If you are one of the unlucky people that has to go on a waiting list, make sure you confirm your interests from time to time so that you keep moving up the list. Allotments can often be quite low down on the list of council priorities, so a gentle reminder will not do any harm.

Another good idea is to get in touch with other like-minded people, as the 1908 Allotments Act states that a council has a duty to provide a sufficient number of allotments when requested by letter from 'six resident registered parliamentary electors or rate payers'. If enough of you get together and request allotment plots, it might just jolt the council into taking action to find fresh sites.

If you know of any waste land in your area, it might be worth approaching the council to see if it is possible to have this turned into a cultivated site. Many farmers are now prepared to lease portions of their land, as they are finding it harder and harder to make ends meet.

On the Isle of Wight there is an innovative scheme in operation called Adopt-A-Garden. Householders no longer able or willing to tend their own garden are teamed with someone who wants a growing space. The householder gets a well-kept and productive garden, and the gardener gets a free 'allotment'. No money exchanges hands and the contract can be reviewed at any time provided either party gives one month's notice.

Take the initiative and rent an allotment and discover all the benefits it can bring – an affordable source of fruit and vegetables; no hidden pesticides or chemicals; plenty of fresh air and exercise; reduction in stress; a renewed sense of achievement and meeting new friends.

CHOOSING A PLOT

When you reach the top of the list and you receive the letter saying you can now have an allotment, you will probably be offered a choice of plots. If you are in the lucky position to be able to choose then there are a few points to consider:

• Have you got the time to take on a full-size plot, or would a half plot be more realistic? Remember that the traditional plot is 10 square rods, or in layman terms 253 square metres. This can amount to a lot of work, particularly if the plot has not been tended for a long time.

• If the plot has been left unattended for several months then it is going to be covered in weeds. You will need to assess what type of weeds they are and the extent of infestation. Not all weeds are bad news, though. If there are brambles, nettles and a few annual weeds, this would indicate that the soil is still fertile and would be relatively easy to deal with. If, however, the plot is infested with perennial weeds that have rhizomes or fleshy roots – ground elder being a prime example – then bear in mind these types of weeds are very hard to eradicate. Cultivating the soil can make the problem worse.

• Take a look at the neighbouring plots. If they are not well tended and covered with weeds, then you will probably find your newly cultivated plot would be plagued by seeds from these plots.

• Is the plot easy to access? If you want to transport a significant amount of manure, a rotovator or a shed to the plot, you need to ask yourself how you would get these things to the plot.

• Make sure there is an adequate water supply at the site. You will spend a lot of your time watering, so you don't want to be carrying water long distances. Water butts are great, so if you decide to erect a shed, incorporate a water butt to collect excess water from the roof when it rains.

• Regrettably vandalism can be a problem in some areas. If the allotment is overlooked by a busy road or neighbours, it is probably less likely to be attacked than one that is hidden out of sight.

• Most crops require plenty of sunshine, so try to avoid a plot that is sheltered by large trees. Small hedges and trees are fine, as they will afford shelter from strong winds. If you do wish to grow some plants that prefer shady conditions, you can easily get round the problem by planting taller plants to provide shade.

- Try and choose a plot that has recently been tended, because you should find it much easier to manage. Unless you are very unlucky the previous gardener will already have done some of the hard work by getting the soil in good shape and ready for planting.

- Check that the paths between each plot are wide enough and firm enough to negotiate with a wheelbarrow. You and your immediate neighbours will be responsible for keeping the paths around your plot mowed and free of weeds.

- Make sure the plot is on level ground. If it is on a slope this means a lot of hard work, as you will have to terrace everything to prevent the soil constantly slipping downhill.

If you are in the enviable position of being able to choose not just the plot, but the allotment site as well, then you might like to consider the following:

- Find out if the allotment is on a statutory site. A statutory site is one that has been acquired specifically for use as allotments and cannot be sold or used for other purposes without the consent of the Secretary of State. Allotments that are privately owned or only on a temporary lease are not protected in the same way.

- Does the site have an allotment society?

You usually find that the sites that have a well-organized society or committee where each plot holder can have a say in running the site, have better facilities. The rules will vary from society to society, but the allotments are usually required to be kept to a certain standard, making the whole site much nicer to work in.

- Check out what security measures are in place at the site. Some may be fenced all round with a lock and key, while others are open to all and sundry. If the site is in the middle of a built-up area, adequate security is essential, and if it is not safely locked at night, you would be well advised to look for a plot elsewhere.

- Some sites have facilities such as toilets, a club house, communal sheds and a tool-share option in place. If you are lucky enough to come across one of these sites, jump at the chance to take a plot as soon as possible.

Having chosen your plot, or at least narrowed your choice down, the final test is to check the state of the soil. Take a spade and dig a hole to a depth below the level of the topsoil. The next layer, or subsoil, will give you an indication of what the drainage is like. If the soil is heavy clay then the chances are that the plot could become waterlogged over winter.

To learn more about soil conditions see pages 42–44.

Tools of the Trade

GARDEN TOOLS

Most gardeners take pleasure in building up a collection of tools with which to perform all the necessary tasks with the minimum of effort. A good tool doesn't have to cost a fortune. Many treasured favourites are family heirlooms or those bought very reasonably at flea markets and car-boot fairs.

Before buying any tool make sure that it is man enough for the job. Even some of the more expensive gardening implements can be quite weak at the joints, only lasting one or two seasons before breaking. Handle them and make sure they feel right for your height and size. Wood handles are strong and warm to the touch, but if weight is an issue then you could go for tools with strong polypropylene shafts. The internet is a good place to compare prices if you don't have time to go round all the garden centres, but I would still advise taking a note of the make and trying it out first.

FORKS

If you don't buy anything else, buy a digging fork. This is the tool that will do all the backbone of the work. They are used for general cultivation, lifting root crops and shifting manure and bulky compost. A fork will penetrate the soil much easier than a spade, particularly if it is heavy clay or full of stones. Forks are also ideal for removing weeds, as you can lift them up from the roots rather than chopping them up with the blade of a spade. There are two sizes of forks – the standard and the border. If you are very tall you can find one with a longer handle if you search around; this is advisable as you don't want to suffer from constant backache from too much bending.

SPADES

This tool is invaluable for heavy digging, cutting straight edges on your plot, turning your compost heap from one bin to another and transferring topsoil. There are two main types of spade – the standard and the smaller border or ladies' spade. The border spade is designed to be used in confined spaces, but is ideal for people of small stature who struggle with heavier tools. If you can cope with the standard spade then you will find that the heavier blade can make quicker work of a large amount of digging. Again, if you are on the tall side, try to find a spade with a longer shaft to make life easier. Some spades come with a tread on the top of the blade; this makes it easier to push the blade into the soil, but they are usually only found on the more expensive tools. Buy stainless-steel spades and forks, as they don't rust and are by far the easiest to clean. Many of the cheaper tools have carbon steel blades and these will perform well if cleaned regularly and oiled after use.

HOES

Hoes come in many shapes and sizes and are mainly used for weeding. They also serve to aerate the soil, can be used to form seed drills and various other tasks. Controlling weeds with a hoe is far quicker than doing it by hand. Hoes are designed to be used with either a pushing or pulling movement to slice off the roots at just below soil level. Because they are designed to cut, you will need to make sure that you always keep your hoe sharp. Make sure that you stand as upright as possible when using a hoe to make it easy on your back. They key to achieving this is to choose a hoe with the correct length of shaft to suit your height. The top of the handle should be level with your ear when the hoe is upright, with the blade resting on the ground.

The Dutch hoe has a D-shaped blade and is probably the most common type you will see. It is excellent for cutting through surface weeds without damaging plant roots. The draw hoe is ideal for chopping weeds and can also be used to earth up potatoes or for making drills for sewing seeds. The onion hoe is a short-handled draw hoe that is useful for weeding between closely grown rows of plants. This type of hoe is used in a kneeling or squatting position.

Try a few out to find out which sort of hoe suits you best, or if in doubt ask a few of your neighbours on the allotment to see if they have any recommendations.

DIGGING HOES

The digging hoe is also known as the eye hoe, grub hoe or Chillington hoe. Although these are not common in the UK, many allotment gardeners who are lucky enough to own one say they are invaluable for digging over the ground very quickly and with much less effort than with a conventional spade.

It is a totally different action digging with a hoe than with a regular spade. Instead of pushing the blade into the soil, the heavy hoe blade swings down from hip height into the soil using its own weight, the natural force of gravity and a little help from your arms. It means that you can dig in an upright position making it easier on your back. Digging hoes can be used to quickly weed large areas and paths, cultivate land ready for planting and clear coarse weeds and undergrowth. In fact a digging hoe can do everything that a shovel or spade can do with the exception of lifting material into a wheelbarrow or moving large quantities of material to another spot.

TROWELS AND HAND FORKS

If your entire family is planning to help you cultivate the allotment, then it would be a good idea to buy each person their own trowel. They are invaluable for transplanting seedlings and digging small holes and are a great tool for children to use as they are not too big. Hand forks are the same size as trowels but have tines. This tool is great for weeding between seedlings.

RAKES

For allotment gardening you will need to choose a rake with a flat head rather than the type with spindly spokes. The ones with short, wide, rounded teeth are ideal for final soil levelling and producing the fine-soiled beds needed for raising plants from seed. Rakes are also great for drawing up and mounding soil, for pulling out stones and for breaking up small clumps of earth.

HAND CULTIVATOR

This tool looks like a claw with three or five prongs at the end of a shaft or handle. It is used to aerate and break up the surface of the soil, while loosening weeds. There is also the star-wheeled cultivator with four or five stars that rotate on the same axle when pushed and pulled along the soil.

SECATEURS

This is another allotment staple, used to prune the woody stems off fruit canes and remove old flower heads. It is also invaluable for taking cuttings for propagation and lesser tasks, such as cutting up vegetation bound for the compost heap. Make sure you buy a decent pair of secateurs that will last you a long time rather than cheap ones that will break after a year. They are small enough to carry back and forth from your garden to the allotment, so you needn't worry about the risk of them being stolen.

There are two main types of secateurs – by-pass, which cut with a scissor action or anvil secateurs which have one blade cutting against a flat, lower anvil. Go for secateurs that have either stainless-steel or carbon steel blades in preference to coated steel. Make sure they fit your hand comfortably and bear in mind when choosing that those with a ratchet require less effort and cause less strain on your hands.

GARDEN KNIFE

Most experienced gardeners say they would not be without their garden knife. It can be used for harvesting many different types of vegetables, cutting string and many other little tasks that crop up all the time. Take good care of your knife: keep it sharp, dry the blade after use and wipe it over with an oily rag to keep it in good condition.

SCISSORS OR HAND SHEARS

Scissors or hand shears are by far the best tool for cutting salad leaves and herbs. They are also useful for many different tasks, such as cutting string, topiary, dead heading, precision trimming, even of small twigs. They are a great all-rounder, one that you will probably wonder how you ever managed without.

GARDENING BELT OR HOLSTER

You might like to consider buying yourself a gardening belt of holster so that you can keep your secateurs, knife and scissors within easy reach at all times.

WATERING CAN

On many allotment sites there is a restriction or complete ban on using hoses, particularly in times of drought. You will need at least two watering cans, as it is a waste of time and effort walking to the nearest tap with just one can when you have another free hand. The plastic type are lighter when full of water, which makes the load a little lighter if you are not very strong – though hopefully all the digging will have built up your muscles! In addition to the cans themselves you will need a fine or medium rose to water seeds or seedlings.

BUCKETS

It is a good idea to keep a couple of buckets on the site where you are working. These can be used for carrying small tools, cropping, weeding or transporting small amounts of manure or compost.

TRUGS

A traditional, hand-crafted trug made from wood is ideal for carrying hand tools, vegetables and can do most of the jobs a bucket can do with the exception of holding water and other liquids.

The larger, plastic, brightly coloured trugs are also very useful to the gardener and come in an assortment of colours and sizes. They can be moved around easily, are very flexible, can be folded in half to pour liquid contents into a bucket, or stored flat in a shed.

SPRAYERS

Small hand-held sprayers are useful for applying organic mixtures to get rid of aphids. They can also be used to mist spray and water plants.

WATER BUTT

Use a water butt to collect water that falls on your shed and/or greenhouse roof. It will need to be raised off the ground to allow for a watering can to fit beneath the tap at the bottom. The butt should also have a lid to prevent insects and debris from polluting the water and blocking up the tap outlet.

WHEELBARROWS

A wheelbarrow is essential for moving large quantities of manure or compost around your plot. You may also need it to transport plants, crops and tools. The plastic wheelbarrow is lighter than a metal one, but you will need to treat it with more care as they are prone to splitting. Metal wheelbarrows are stronger but are liable to

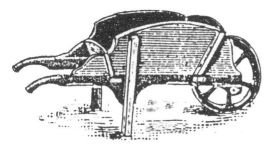

rust. Galvanized steel lasts the longest but they are more expensive. If you need a wheelbarrow for heavy work then it is a good idea to buy one from a builder's merchant or DIY store.

GLOVES

Many gardeners prefer to use their bare hands, saying they can't feel what is going on in the soil if they are wearing gloves. There are occasions, however, when every gardener can use a pair of sturdy gloves, especially when dealing with nettles or very prickly plants. Buy ones that are comfortable and strong enough to prevent pricks and abrasions and make sure they fit properly, as there is nothing worse than having gardening gloves that are too big for your hands.

PLANT LABELS AND MARKER PEN

The white plant labels from garden centres are adequate for the purpose but they can easily get trampled on. You can always make your own from wood offcuts, old lolly sticks or plastic ice-cream-tub lids. You will also need a waterproof marker pen for writing on the labels.

TWINE AND SKEWERS

Make sure you keep a large ball of gardener's twine and a few skewers handy. These can be used for marking straight lines across your plot as a guide when sowing. Twine can also be used to tie climbing plants and to support canes.

GARDENING BAG

A gardening bag is useful if you don't have anywhere to leave your tools overnight. A canvas bag specially designed for this purpose is invaluable for carrying small tools, packets of seeds, gardening gloves and of course the odd snack and bottle of water.

DUSTBIN

It is a good idea to keep a large plastic or metal dustbin on the site for taking anything that cannot go on the compost heap.

DIBBER

A dibber is a pencil-shaped tool used for making planting holes. Have two different sized dibbers – one pencil-sized and one slightly thicker that can be made from a cut-down wooden spade handle.

ADDITIONAL EQUIPMENT

The following equipment is designed to prolong the growing season and also to protect your plants from pests.

CLOCHES

A cloche is used to protect plants and seedlings that need a little extra warmth when the weather is not being very kind. There are a wide variety of cloches – glass, rigid and flexible plastics – available to buy. For the allotment, home-made cloches constructed from recycled materials are ideal. You can make small cloches by cutting off the tops of plastic bottles. Larger ones can be made from old sheets of clear plastic or old glass window panes.

HORTICULTURAL FLEECE

This is a spun fibre similar to cheesecloth, which can be draped over plants as a protection against frost or aphids. It is ideal to use as a 'floating' cloche to cover newly sewn seeds. It has the advantage of allowing rainwater to penetrate the soil, while still insulating the ground. Being so lightweight, the fleece still allows the plants freedom to grow.

POLYTUNNELS

A polytunnel is a structure made out of lightweight polythene film laid over a set of wire hoops. They are designed to protect a row of young plants while they grow and to minimize frost and pest damage. They can also be used to increase heat and humidity for plants that favour these conditions. Some of the sturdier polytunnels will be strong enough to deter birds and rabbits from eating your crop. The advantage of a polytunnel is that it is lightweight and can be moved around easily. They come in all shapes and sizes, from small models designed for home gardeners to much larger ones for commercial use.

COLD FRAMES

Cold frames are bottomless boxes with a sloping, see-through lid that are designed to protect young plants. They are more substantial than cloches and can extend your growing season. They should ideally be placed against a wall with plenty of sun to maximize solar absorption. Placing it on a slight slope with also help with drainage. Make sure it is in a sheltered position; if you sink it into the ground slightly, the earth provides extra insulation. They are reasonably light and portable and, unlike a greenhouse, can be moved around the plot.

MULCH MATERIALS

There are many times when it is handy to have some type of mulching material available. For example, if you have recently harvested a crop but are not ready to plant a new one, covering the ground with a mulch will discourage the growth of weeds. Cardboard, pebbles, gravel, bark chippings, well-rotted manure, old newspapers and leaf mould all make good mulches.

BIODEGRADABLE SHEETING
There are times when you will need to cover quite a large area of soil for weed control, so choose a biodegradable sheeting. This should be compostable and should allow you to keep on top of weeds without having to resort to the use of any chemicals. It can also help to retain the moisture and soil temperature when the ground is not being used.

MESH OR NETTING
Mesh and netting are available in various materials and gauges. They can be used to protect your fruit bushes and trees from birds and rabbits, can act as a support for climbing plants, a windbreak and also for shading greenhouse plants.

SEED TRAYS AND POTS
You can never have too many seed trays and pots for sewing seeds and potting on. It is also a good way of recycling old containers and packaging instead of just throwing them away. Old yoghurt pots and butter containers are ideal for sewing seeds, as long as you make a few holes in the bottom.

AIRTIGHT CONTAINERS
If you have a shed on the site, some resealable containers will come in handy. Not only can you use them to store seeds, but essential tea-break supplies can also be kept there. Biscuit tins are ideal, as they are not only airtight but also mouse-proof.

CHAIR
A lightweight, fold-up chair in your shed gives you somewhere to sit comfortably when you want to take a break.

WATERPROOF CLOTHES
Keeping an old raincoat at the allotment is a good idea in case you get caught out by the weather – a natural hazard of gardening. A spare pair of boots, a pair of sunglasses, a hat and a warm jacket means that you are prepared for all weathers.

PRIMUS STOVE
If you intend to spend a lot of time at the allotment, a small primus stove can come in handy for boiling water. If you don't want to go to that expense, you can always take a thermos flask with you.

WOOD
A plank of wood at least 1.5 metres long and 30 cm wide is useful when you want to plant. You can lay this between your rows to stand on and it will also give you a straight line to follow. If you want to get really technical you can use a waterproof marker and mark a wooden batten with 10 cm intervals to give you a useful spacer for planting.

MAINTENANCE OF TOOLS

Even though most gardeners are full of good intentions when they first acquire their set of new tools, many fail to keep them in tip-top condition. This is often because they are too tired after a long session at the allotment, or it just slips their mind as they go home armed with a basket full of goodies. If you can get into the habit of regularly cleaning and oiling your tools, you will find it very satisfying when you return to find them hanging up in an orderly fashion without a spot of mud on them.

If you are really too tired to clean and sharpen them at the end of the day, a temporary solution is to keep a bucket full of sand with a little oil added to it in the corner of your shed. Just before you leave dip the blades of your tools in the sand; not only will it remove the worst of the dirt, it will also give them a nice coating of oil.

Wooden shafts will usually remain in fairly good condition, as your hands contain a certain amount of oils, but they will always benefit from a rub down and a coating of oil once they have dried. Linseed oil is probably the best, but any vegetable oil will serve the purpose.

SHARPENING

Even the most expensive garden tool is rendered useless if it is allowed to go blunt. The traditional way of keeping tools sharp is to use a sharpening or whetstone. Oil the blade first then push the blade away from you as you rub it in a circular movement across the surface of the stone. Try to keep it at a constant angle and only apply a slight downward pressure. You will find it easier to move the stone over the blade on larger tools, such as hoes and spades. It might take you a while to get used to using a whetstone, but once you have mastered the action you will achieve good results.

For smaller blades, such as those on scissors, secateurs or gardening knives, you might find it easier to buy a proprietary sharpener, sometimes referred to as diamond sharpeners. To sharpen a pair of secateurs, place the sharpener with the upright single bevel level. Then stroke gently to sharpen along the curve of the blade, always moving towards the outside of the tool. Clean the blade and test for sharpness by cutting on a branch or plant.

POTS AND PROPAGATORS

It isn't just the tools that need to be kept clean; pots, propagators, labels and plant trays need to be maintained regularly. At the end of the season when the mad growing panic has slowed down, do an annual check of all your equipment. Any cracked or broken terracotta pots can be recycled; break them up and use the fragments in the bottom of larger pots to create good drainage.

Wait for a nice sunny day, then wash all your labels, pots, cloches and trays in a bucket of warm water with a little environmentally friendly washing-up liquid. Allow them to dry off in the sun, then put them away for the winter, knowing that they will be free from diseases and ready for the next growing season.

MAKE YOUR OWN

Garden shops and catalogues are full of little gadgets for the keen gardener, but many of these things are just luxuries and you can easily make do with some recycled object. For example, you can easily make plant pots out of old newspapers. Herbs, such as parsley, do not like to be transplanted, so using a biodegradable pot made out of newspaper solves the problem. The newspaper will simply rot away and the roots will grow through the newspaper. You can buy fancy kits to do this, but a simple glass jar, some newspaper and your usually potting mixture is all you need.

Method

1. Fold a single sheet of newspaper in the centre fold, then fold again until you have a long, narrow piece of paper. The width of the paper should be the height of your jar.

2. Roll the jar up inside the newspaper keeping the paper as flat as possible, then simple pull out the jar leaving the roll of newspaper intact.

3. Tuck the newspaper into itself to make it secure.

4. To make the base of the pot, tear half a sheet of newspaper into four pieces. Standing your newspaper tube on its end so that it is resting on the table, stuff the four pieces of paper into the bottom and press it down hard using the jar.

5. If you want to make the pots really secure, you can tie a piece of string around each one, or alternatively pack them together tightly on a tray.

6. Now fill with potting compost and plant your seeds just as you would in a normal plant pot. The newspaper will stand gentle watering until the seedling is large enough to plant out. The newspaper will gradually rot away in the earth without disturbing the roots of the plant.

Plastic drinks bottles have numerous uses for the gardener. They can be used as a sleeve around plants, such as lettuces, to keep slugs and snails from eating the young leaves. They can be put on top of the canes that support your plants so that there is no risk of anyone poking their eye out. They can be hung up as bird scarers or placed neck down in the soil with their bottoms cut off to act as funnels to direct water to the roots of a plant. They are also very useful left intact for storing home-made liquid fertilizer.

SHEDS AND GREENHOUSES

It is difficult to imagine an allotment plot without a shed, somehow the two just seem to go together. Often they can appear quite ramshackle and eccentric, as the keen DIYer has made one out of recycled materials with great ingenuity and imagination.

You might be lucky enough to find a plot that already has a shed in situ; if not, the positioning of this vital piece of equipment is your first priority. Before you rush out and buy a shed you will need to contact your allotment association to find out if there are any restrictions regarding buildings on your plot. They will often have rules regarding the size, materials used, the position and the number of constructions on any one site.

If you are allowed to put up a reasonably sized construction, then plan it carefully. You will want it large enough to store tools and other sundry items, such as seed trays and pots, cloches and fleece, twine and labels and whatever else you know you will be using on a regular basis. You may wish to duplicate some of your tools so that you are not carrying them permanently from home to your allotment. The shed is also a place to shelter from bad weather and somewhere to take a well-earned break from your hard work.

It might be worth waiting until there is a sale at your local DIY store. If you have plenty of time you might like to build your own sturdy shed using recycled materials. This can of course save you quite a lot of money and reduce your carbon footprint at the same time. I have seen sheds made from redundant horse trailers, pieces of old corrugated iron and one ingenious man took an old fishing boat apart and made a magnificent structure.

If the idea of making a shed appeals to you, then old wooden pallets work very well. There are often pallets lying around outside factories and warehouses and, in many cases, these are surplus to requirements. It is worth approaching the company to see if they have any to spare. You can use this pallet-wood to strengthen an existing shed, as part of a new build or for the entire shed.

If theft and vandalism are common at your site, you will need to think seriously about how you will make your shed as secure as possible. Even if the shed cost you very little, it is worth buying a really good-quality closed-shackle padlock. This should be attached to a hasp on a secure mounting point, with the hasp itself having concealed fixings or recessed bolts. Alternatively you could fit a mortice-style lock designed specifically for sheds. Many of the sheds you find for sale at DIY and garden centres can be rather flimsy, so you might like to consider strengthening these with some recycled timber. It is usually the window that is the weakest point of the structure, so consider putting some type of removable shuttering on the inside to provide additional security.

Do not position your shed in a place where it is out of view, because this means it is easier for someone to break into it without being spotted. Don't keep anything in the shed that is really valuable, or anything that you really do not want to lose. Many allotment gardeners keep a spare set of less expensive tools in their shed. Car-boot fairs are a great place to find inexpensive tools.

GREENHOUSES

Again, as in acquiring a shed, you will need to consult the regulations as to whether you are allowed to put a greenhouse on your plot. You might find that you are allowed one or the other, but not both.

If you are allowed to erect a greenhouse, you will be extending your growing season considerably. It will provide an environment to bring on young plants and to grow tomatoes, peppers, cucumbers and grapes. During the winter you will be able to continue growing a variety of salad crops, such as winter lettuce, rocket, parsley and radishes.

The downside, if you consider this a problem, is that a greenhouse will mean you have more jobs to do and will have to visit the allotment more frequently. To keep pests and diseases to a minimum, your greenhouse will require regular cleaning and should be kept free of dead leaves. At least once a year, preferably on a mild day in early winter, clean and disinfect the entire greenhouse. The glass can be cleaned with a proprietary window cleaner and you will find a thin plastic plant label is ideal for cleaning the gaps between the panes. Shelves and other surfaces should be sterilized using a garden disinfectant.

The greenhouse should be positioned in a light position away from large trees, but in a sheltered spot away from the wind. Gardening experts usually advise that your greenhouse should be positioned with its ridge running from east to west, taking advantage of the best light down one side of the structure. Make sure when choosing the spot that at least one part of one side or even the back end of the greenhouse captures as much of the light from the south as possible. This sunlight will be very beneficial to the growth of young plants.

The next thing to consider is the position of any trees. It is not a good idea to place a greenhouse directly under a tree, as this will probably keep it in shade for most of the day. You need to bear in mind that the sun is low in the sky during the spring and winter months, so you don't want anything that will cast shadows. If you don't take advantage of the best light possible, your seedlings will become leggy and you will not end up with very strong plants.

If you feel a new greenhouse is too expensive, you might like to consider getting a second-hand one. You can often find advertisements in your local paper, or reycling web sites offer them free if you are prepared to collect them. When buying a second-hand greenhouse, it is best to go for one with an aluminium frame, as these are much easier to dismantle, transport and reassemble. If you do have a choice, opt for polycarbonate panes rather than glass, as these will be much safer if your allotment is subject to vandalism.

Heating your greenhouse

Because the British climate can be a little unpredictable, growing plants in an unheated greenhouse can be a bit of a gamble. Although the building itself will act as a solar trap, on dull chilly days and at night when temperatures can plummet, tender plants can easily become damaged. Because it is unlikely that you will have any access to electricity and gas heaters can be hazardous if left unattended, it is worth considering the passive method of heating. The passive method uses natural heat sources that absorb heat during the day, then circulates the heat during the colder nights. However, because this method takes advantage of the heat of the sun during the day, you might find that the colder winter months will not generate enough heat for it to be successful.

To create a passive form of heating you will need to have a heat sink that will absorb the heat during the day. You can create a heat sink by using:

- rocks, paving slabs or concrete blocks held together in a metal cage;

- large, plastic water or disused food barrels.

- a 'hot bed' of compost or well-rotted manure.

To improve the performance of the heat sink it is advisable to coat the objects with a non-reflective black paint, because this will increase their ability to asborb heat. Make sure you place the sink in a position where it will catch the maximum amount of sunlight. Also make sure it is away from the

sides of the greenhouse. The reason for this is that the panes of glass will quickly absorb the heat once the outside temperature drops if the heat sink is allowed to come into contact with the panes.

The downside to this type of heating is that it can take up quite a lot of precious space inside the greenhouse, but it is worth it if your plants get the benefit of extra warmth.

If you are using compost or manure, it is important to ensure this is turned regularly in order to maintain the temperature and keep the bed truly 'hot'.

If you really want to retain the warmth inside the greenhouse, you could insulate the glass using bubble wrap until the danger of cold nights has passed. Also make sure that the greenhouse is as airtight as possible. Remember, though, do not cover all of the vents because winter ventilation is required for humidity control and to restore the oxygen/carbon dioxide balance in the greenhouse. Keep these vents in good

working condition so that they close tightly when they are not in use.

Passive heating has been used in the UK for many years and proved very successful in large Victorian hothouses. It is certainly worth trying because, as well as costing very little, harnessing the power of the sun to help your plants develop will prove your ecological credentials.

Finally, you must make sure you prepare your greenhouse for the winter months by sealing every nook and cranny. Vents and doors should be weather-stripped, cracks must be caulked and should be checked every year for wear and tear. A really good way of checking to see if you have any leaks is to go inside the greenhouse, close the door and any vents and light an incense stick. Hold the smoking stick up to any places you suspect might not be airtight, and you will be able to see the smoke respond to the incoming air currents. Remember, one small leak can make all the difference.

Planning and Preparation

PREPARING THE SITE

It is the first time you have visited your allotment since signing the necessary forms and all of a sudden the enormity of the task in front of you seems overwhelming! You don't know where to start and you are wondering whether you have made a mistake. This chapter aims to break the preparation down into simple, manageable tasks.

If your site is a huge pile of rubble or overrun with weeds, don't be put off; even the most overgrown site can be tamed with a little bit of work and determination. Take a deep breath, plan carefully how much time you want to spend and tackle the site a little at a time. There are times when you might feel like giving up, particularly if your neighbour's plot is pristine with immaculately tilled rows, but don't be discouraged – you will get there!

Instead of thinking of the plot as a whole, why not break it down into four separate beds. Even if you don't manage to clear the entire site before the start of the growing season, you can get a few of your favourite vegetables planted on a portion of the ground.

As the site starts to take shape you will find that you become addicted to the fresh air, the enthusiasm of the other gardeners and the drive to plant and eventually eat your own fresh produce.

WEEDS

If your plot is overrun with weeds you will need to identify what type they are and take appropriate action.

Perennial weeds

The perennial weeds include cough grass, bindweed, creeping thistle, docks and ground elder. If you know that you have perennial weeds do not attempt to rotovate the soil, as this will simply spread the problem. Either deprive the weeds of light for a season by covering them with a sheet of heavy, black plastic or dig the plants out carefully, making sure you get all the roots.

Annual weeds

These are much easier to control by hoeing, hand-weeding or mulching. Just make sure you pull them up before you start planting.

Grass

If you need to remove grass, simply take off the turf and turn it upside down and bury it to about a spade's depth. Cover it with topsoil and it will rot down to produce beneficial loam.

USING A ROTOVATOR

Many newcomers to gardening are keen to get their plot cleared and will resort to hiring or borrowing a rotovator to turn the entire plot. This is not always a good idea. Many weeds are able to grow back vigorously from just a tiny fragment of their roots, so chopping them up and tilling the soil is the perfect way to ensure that your plot will be covered in lush weeds in just a few weeks time.

There is no doubt a rotovator is a good tool for breaking up heavily compacted soil, but you will need to deal with the problem of the weeds first. It is not advisable to contaminate the soil with systemic weedkillers, so tackle a small part of the plot at a time and dig up the weeds, making sure you take out all of the roots.

To keep the rest of the plot under control until you are ready to cultivate it, use sheet mulches of layers of newspaper, cardboard or black plastic sheeting. Once you have cleared each section of weeds, you can then turn it over using a rotovator, incorporating rotted manure or compost at the same time.

DIGGING BY HAND

Digging by hand, fork or digging hoe will improve the condition of the soil for plant growth by aerating the ground. If the soil is heavy it will also improve the drainage and structure of the soil. The best time to dig over the plot is autumn, as the winter frosts will help to break down any remaining large clumps of earth. It is not advisable to dig heavy soil when it is wet, as this will only damage the structure of the soil. There are a number of different methods to choose from when digging:

• Single digging

This, as the name implies, is lifting a spadeful of soil, turning it and dropping it back into the same spot. Weeds can be removed and organic matter added as required.

• Double digging

This is a more methodical approach where a plot is dug over to a spade's depth (or 'spit') one trench after another. Start at one end and dig out the first trench, taking the soil to the far end of the trench in a wheelbarrow. Break up the newly revealed subsoil with a fork. Move on to the next section, dig up the top soil, remove any weeds and put the soil back in the first trench with some compost or manure. Work your way down the entire length of the plot, removing any weeds and roots and putting the soil from the wheelbarrow into the last trench. Try to avoid mixing any of the topsoil with the subsoil.

• No digging

If your ground is in good condition and free of pernicous weeds, then there is no need to dig at all and you can get the worms to do the work for you. Put a good layer of well-rotted compost on the beds during the autumn. The worms will take this down for you in vertical channels that help to aerate the soil and deliver water to the roots of your plants. In the spring, give the soil a good rake.

SOIL ADDITIVES

If you want to get the best out of your plants, they need a soil with good structure that contains all the necessary nutrients. A well-structured soil is not compacted and has enough space for air, water and nutrients to circulate. In nature compost is made naturally, as plants and creatures die and rot down to build up a rich, fertile soil. As a gardener we need to replicate this natural process by adding our own nutrients to the soil. Organic matter, including well-rotted manure and garden compost will help to improve the structure of the soil

and also provides nutrients. There are other additives you can use but these will depend on the type of soil on your allotment. Poor drainage in a heavy clay soil can be improved with gravel, grit or sharp sand but it would require a large quantity to make a difference.

Manure

Manure not only adds nutrients but its bulky nature also improves the structure of the soil. If the structure of the soil is right, then the plant's roots are able to absorb nutrients more readily. Natural manures also come with the added benefit of micronutrients that might not be present in an inorganic fertilizer.

When you first start to cultivate your plot, manure is probably the best thing to add to your soil, as your compost heap will not be ready to use for a few months.

Manure must be well rotted before it is added to the soil, as fresh manure will burn the plants and actually creates a nitrogen deficiency while it is rotting down. This is especially true of horse manure, as it often contains bedding materials, such as straw or sawdust, which have not broken down. When buying manure, try to make sure it comes from an organic source because you would not want to use material that has been contaminated with chemicals.

Garden compost

One of the first things to position on your new site is your compost bin or heap. It will

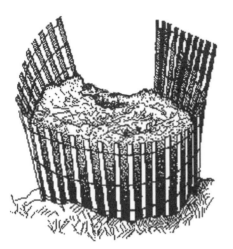

freely and prevent the mixture from becoming too compacted. Regular turning of the compost heap with a garden fork – at least once or twice a month – speeds up the whole composting process. The majority of your waste from the allotment can be composted, but make sure you do not add any pernicious, perennial or annual weeds that have gone to seed.

The compost should be ready to use in about three months. You will know when it is well-rotted because it will be crumbly and brown, damp but not wet, and it should have a pleasant smell. Sieve through the compost with a garden fork and take out any material that has not broken down. This can be put to one side and chopped up with a spade and added to the next batch of compost.

The best way to use compost is to dig it into the plant or vegetable beds; this will improve the soil's texture and provide a long-lasting supply of nutrients. Alternatively you could you it as a mulch, if you have enough.

take a while for your heap to start producing, but the efforts in the long run will be well worth the effort. Try to position your bin or heap in a sunny, sheltered position, as the warmth of the sun will speed up the maturing process. Compost bins are available from DIY stores, garden centres and sometimes local authorities offer them at discounted rates.

It is very easy to make your own. For a simple and quick bin, hammer four wooden stakes into the ground 1 metre apart to form a square. Attach wire or plastic netting around the stakes and line it with cardboard.

The key to making good compost is to make sure that plenty of air can circulate through the material. By using a mixture of finer materials, such as grass clippings and leaves, with coarser materials, such as shrub clippings and straw, the air will circulate

Mushroom compost

If you have a really heavy soil, then spent mushroom compost will help to lighten it, and the lime it contains will reduce the acidity. It is possible to buy in certain garden centres, but it will be cheaper if you can buy it directly from a local mushroom farm.

Green manures

Green manures are fast-growing plants put in the ground for between six weeks and one year then dug back into the soil to provide nutrients. While these plants are growing they help to suppress weeds and are a good idea for any areas that are vacant between crops. There are green manures that are suitable for both summer and winter planting. Some green manures have root systems that will break up heavy ground, others store nitrogen in their roots, which can be released to benefit other plants. Green manures need to be dug into the soil before they go to seed and when the stems are still soft, usually a couple of weeks before the ground is needed. If you are using green manure in a rotation system, Red Clover, for example, being a legume, would fit into a rotation in place of beans and could be followed by a leafy vegetable, such as spinach or lettuce. The added advantage of clover is that its flowers attract bees.

Summer green manures include mustard and rape. These crops will be ready to dig into the ground four to six weeks after sowing.

Winter-specific green manures include grazing rye, winter tare and winter field beans, all of which are good at supplying nitrogen and make good ground cover.

Concentrated organic fertilizers

Bone meal, seaweed meal and blood, fish and bone are concentrated organic fertilizers. They are easy to use and store and this type of fertilizer releases its nutrients slowly.

Leaf mould

Although leaf mould does not supply a great deal of nourishment to the ground, it can help to improve the structure of the soil. Make a cage out of chicken wire and collect the autumn leaves as they fall. Leave them in the cage and allow them to rot for about a year. When ready, the leaves will become a pleasant, dark brown, crumbly material that can also be used as a lawn conditioner and mulch or added to seed and potting mixes.

Lime

Certain types of vegetable require lime if they are being grown in a particularly acidic soil. Lime can be spread on the soil at any time of year, but it needs to be done well in advance of planting if possible. Make sure you do not add lime when you are digging in manure, as the two can react against each other. It is best to apply lime and manure in different years, depending on your crop rotation plan. If your soil is not too acidic, mushroom compost is a more gentle way of raising the pH levels.

PLANNING THE BEDS

Raised beds are a great way to start laying out your allotment, especially if you are in an area with heavy soil and poor drainage. The idea is to set up a series of permanent rectangular growing areas that are intersected by paths. This means every part of the bed is accessible without you having to stand on the soil. Raised beds allow you to start growing vegetables immediately and extend your growing time, as the soil is higher up and warms up earlier.

The key to raised beds is to keep them simple. Make between four and eight beds and rotate them in the same way you would crops in the ground. They need to be deep enough for you to work comfortably without straining your back – 1.2 metres is normal, but you can go as deep as 1.5 metres if you wish.

Fork over the ground to loosen any weeds and stones, then rake it flat. Mark out the shapes of your beds using twine and skewers. The easiest way of containing the soil within the beds is to make an edging using pressure-treated planks or old floorboards. These should be slightly higher than the level of the topsoil so that the soil does not wash away in a heavy downpour. Then fill the beds with topsoil, which you could get delivered to the site, or buy bags of organic planting material from a garden centre, which will cost you a lot more.

If you decide you don't want to go to the trouble of making raised beds, it is a good idea to plan the layout of your allotment on a piece of paper first. Mark where you will have your compost heap, your greenhouse and/or shed, your seed beds, your fruit bushes and so on. It is still a good idea to have paths between your beds to give you easy access for working. This will save you time on digging in the long run because the soil in which your crops will actually grow won't become so compacted.

Once you have worked out where to put the more permanent features on your allotment and designed where the paths will go, your next step is to put the plants into their specific groups.

ANNUAL VEGETABLES

Choose a site for your annual vegetables, which will need the sunniest part of your allotment. They do all their growing in one season and will need the best conditions. To work a rotation scheme (see page 40) you will need at least four beds – raised ones work really well because the soil will be both rich and deep.

PERMANENTS

You will need to leave space for any permanent crops, such as an asparagus bed which will give you delicious spears for about 20 years. Then there will be fruit canes, trees, if you have room, a strawberry bed and seed beds for bringing on young plants.

PERENNIALS AND HERB BEDS

Any space left over should be used for permanent perennials, flowers and a herb garden. Because salad leaves don't like to be in full sunlight, these can be slotted in between the slower-growing crops that can help provide some shade.

WILDLIFE CORNER

Remember that the best friend of the organic gardener is natural wildlife. To encourage wildlife onto your plot, you can leave a corner of your ground undisturbed, with, say, a few logs and a couple of rocks to encourage insects to make their homes. If you leave a little verge of uncut grass you will be encouraging insects, centipedes and other beneficial insects that will help to keep the unwanted pests at bay. Finally plant some flowers in your beds to attract hoverflies, ladybirds and lacewings, which are all great at getting rid of pests. Marigolds, nasturtiums, poached-egg plant, fennel, angelica and dill are great for this. Bees, or the pollinators, are attracted by vegetables and herbs, particularly mint, lavender and thyme.

It is a good idea to allow some of your flowers to go to seed to give the birds some food during the winter months. They also love berries and rosehips, but you might need to cover your fruit bushes to stop them stealing your crop.

CROP ROTATION

The principle of crop rotation is to grow specific groups of vegetables on a different piee of land every year. These groups are moved around so that they do not grow in the same spot for at least three years. Many people who are starting out ignore the rotation system, but in the long term you will derive better results from your efforts if you stick to the basic principle. The idea is to reduce the build-up of diseases, thereby reducing the need for chemicals. Also, certain vegetables add nutrients to the soil, making it better for the next season's crop.

There are four groups of vegetables to rotate – potatoes, legumes, brassicas, and onions and root vegetables. You will need to have four separate beds to accommodate these groups. By using this method you need only apply manure to one quarter of the ground each year and that will be in the bed where you are growing the potatoes. The grouping is designed to meet the needs of each specific family – for example, onion and root vegetables can survive with little water unlike the legumes, which need constant watering.

• Potato family

This group also includes tomatoes, aubergines and peppers. Because members of the potato family benefit from the addition of organic matter, this will benefit the legume family the following year.

• Legumes

These are the plants with pods – for example, peas, broad beans, French and runner beans, sugar snap and mange-tout. These love rich soil, so the heavy manuring left from the potato crop the previous year is perfect. They don't like too much acid, so apply some lime or calcified seaweed before planting. When harvesting legumes, try and leave some of their roots in the ground, as these are a valuable source of nitrogen for the next crop – the brassicas.

• Brassicas

This group includes broccoli, cabbages, Brussels sprouts, Chinese cabbage, radishes, cauliflower, turnips, swedes and kohlrabi. This group will benefit from the lime from the year before, as it is beneficial against club root. They will also benefit from the nitrogen produced by the legume roots that have been left in the ground. Because some of these varieties can grow quite tall, try not to disturb the soil too much by digging. Add some general fertilizer such as blood, fish and bone or bone meal.

• Onions and root vegetables

This group includes all types of onions, chives, garlic, leeks and shallots, as well as carrots, parsnips, celery and celeriac. The beetroot family, which includes beetroot, spinach, Swiss chard and spinach beet make good companions and can go in the same bed. This group likes soil that has been fertilized for a previous crop, so they benefit from the feeding you gave to the brassicas in the previous season. Root crops do not need fresh manure and very little watering. They have been grouped with the onion family because they have very similar requirements.

NON-ROTATION CROPS

These crops are undemanding and can be slotted in anywhere to fill gaps. They include chard, beetroot and spinach, which will benefit from manure but do not depend on it to survive. Lettuces and salad leaves do not have any specific requirements, but will benefit from a little organic matter to lighten and enrich the soil. Crops such as parsley, chives, rocket, dill and coriander can be sown in rows in any free space and do not have any special requirements.

Marrows, pumpkins and courgettes need a soil that can retain water, and will benefit from well-rotted manure put in the base of the planting hole.

Sweetcorn is probably the least demanding of any of the crops, so you can grow this in any of the four beds described above.

THE SOIL

You will need to know about the different types of soil to grow vegetables successfully. There are a few simple tests you can perform to ascertain whether your soil is acid or alkline and, once you know its character, you can make the necessary adjustments to improve it. When you take on your allotment, try to gauge what type of soil you will be dealing with. If the plot if covered with weeds, especially stinging nettles, this would indicate quite a high level of fertility. Take a spade and dig a few holes to see if there is a good number of worms. If there are plenty and they are nice and pink in colour then you are off to a good start. You can also tell quite a lot from the feel of the soil:

• Clay

Clay will feel sticky to the touch and if rolled between the palm of your hands will keep its shape. On the plus side, clay soil can be extremely rich in minerals and retains water and nutrients. On the downside, it doesn't drain well, is slow to warm up in summer and can become very hard in hot weather. If you know your site has clay soil, then raised beds would be the answer, as treading on this type of soil will only make things worse. You can improve the drainage and general texture of clay soil

by digging in plenty of sand or grit and lots of organic matter.

• Chalk

Chalky soil will not keep its shape and is generally full of flintstones. It drains well and contains a lot of lime, which means it is alkaline and not suitable for many plants. Again, consider using raised beds, or alternatively add a lot of humus. (Humus is a sweet-smelling material that is the end product of a long decomposition process.)

• Loam

A loamy soil is made up of sand, silt and clay and is the easiest to work with. If you take a lump in your hands it will take an imprint and break into crumbs. It is dark brown and contains a good mixture of nutrients.

• Sand

Soil that contains a lot of sand will feel gritty and will not hold a shape. Although it is free draining and easy to work with, its main drawback is that its coarse texture allows rainwater to drain through fast, thereby leaching it of essential nutrients and moisture. The plus side of sandy soil is that it warms up quickly and is perfect for sowing seeds directly into the ground. You can help it to retain moisture and nutrients by adding humus, or cover the surface in winter to reduce the nutrients from being washed away.

• Peat

Peat is very dark and spongy but does not keep its shape. It is rich in organic matter and, although fertile, it is very low in minerals. It is easy to work with but can dry out very quickly and has a high acid content. This can be counteracted by adding some lime.

TOPSOIL AND SUBSOIL

Topsoil, as its name suggests, is the top layer of soil. In some places it may only be a few millimetres thick, while in deep river valleys and coastal plains it can be up to several metres. It is usually darker than the subsoil because it has a higher organic content. It is therefore usually lighter and easier to handle than the subsoil beneath it. The subsoil is usually lighter in colour, is stickier to the touch and less fertile. Even though subsoils are not as full of nutrients as the topsoil, they are fairly easy to improve.

ACID SOIL

If the soil contains too much acid, the bacteria present become less active; an indication of this is moss growing on the surface of the soil. These bacteria are essential for breaking down the organic matter into humus. If there is evidence of worm activity and your plants are doing well, then you needn't take any action. If things are not going too well, you can neutralize the acid by adding a little lime. Do not add too much, however, as this could easily upset the fine balance of other nutrients within the soil.

ALKALINE SOIL

If the soil is too alkaline your crops will not do well, as they will be starved of essential nutrients. To redress the balance, dig in loads of organic matter, especially pine needles. Other organic soil additions that can help to acidify soil include oak leaves, leaf mould, peat moss and composted sawdust, all of which will help the soil to retain moisture.

TESTING THE SOIL

To test the pH levels of your soil you will need a soil-testing kit. These are relatively cheap and are available in garden centres. The scale reads from 0 to 14, with the best reading for plant growth being between pH 5.5 to pH 7.5. A pH of 7 is neutral, above 7 is alkaline and below 7 is acid.

Collect three to four samples from various parts of your plot and test them for their pH levels. If the soil is too acid, add lime. If the soil is too alkaline, garden manure and compost should redress the balance. Only add nutrients if they are really necessary, as too much can actually produce toxic results.

Testing the texture

Now that you have ascertained the pH level of your soil you might like to carry out a simple test to find out its texture.

1. Gather some soil from the plot taking some from the surface to a depth of around 20 cm. Leave it to dry in a warm place and then grind it into fine granules in a pestle and mortar.

2. Put a layer about 2.5 cm deep into the bottom of a glass jar. Add a ¼ teaspoon of powdered dishwasher detergent or the type of detergent that will not foam up. Add water until the jar is two thirds full.

3. Shake the jar for a minute, turning it upside down to get all the soil off the bottom. Leave the jar on a shelf or worktop where it can sit undisturbed.

4. After about 5 minutes, mark the level of settled particles on the side of the jar using a crayon or felt-tip pen. This is sand.

5. Now set a timer for four hours. When the alarm goes off, mark the next layer. This is the silt.

6. Leave it for another couple of days to give the clay time to settle, allowing you to take the final measurement.

The measurements on the side of the jar will show the relative percentages of sand, silt and clay, indicating the texture of your soil.

Testing for drainage

Even the most sophisticated tests cannot give you a better result than this simple test. Dig a hole, fill it with water, and simply watch how quickly the water is absorbed.

The following scale will give you an indication as to how well your soil will drain:

- 1 to 12 minutes – the soil is likely to be dry.

- 12 to 30 minutes – the soil has perfect drainage.

- 30 minutes to 4 hours – the drainage is rather slow, but good for plants that like moist conditiions.

- Over 4 hours – drainage is poor and your soil needs help.

The Gardener's Calendar

MONTH-BY-MONTH GUIDE

This section is designed to help you to plan your tasks for the year ahead. You may need to adapt your calendar slightly depending on where you live – for example, Scotland would be a lot colder than the West Country, and their winters generally arrive a lot earlier.

With careful planning there is no reason why you can't enjoy the benefits of your hard work all year round. Remember, if it is a month where there is a lot to do, you are not only saving money but you are benefitting from the freshest possible produce. Also bear in mind that cloches, horticultural fleeces and greenhouses can help you to extend your seasons.

JANUARY

Although the soil is too wet and cold for much planting outdoors, there are still some jobs you can be getting on with both indoors and out.

Sow under protection
Early radishes, broad beans, leeks, lettuces and rocket.

Plant direct
Currants, raspberries and shallot sets.

Crop
Cabbages, leeks, kale, parsnips, broccoli or purple sprouting, cauliflower, celeriac, Jerusalem artichokes, lettuce, radishes, rocket, spinach and Swiss chard.

Other jobs to do
• Purchase and chit seed potatoes.

• Put netting over currant bushes to stop birds eating the new growth.

• Protect any plants from the cold and make sure your cold frames, cloches and fleeces are securely pegged down.

• Force rhubarb by placing an upturned bucket or wooden box over the them, or alternatively surround the crowns with straw.

- Search through your seed catalogues and start planning your beds for the year ahead. Order seeds for spring sowing.

- If you have a rabbit-proof fence around your plot, check for any holes and repair.

- If you have any wayward brambles on your patch, warm yourself up by digging them up.

FEBRUARY

February can still be very cold, but you will notice that the evenings are starting to get a little bit lighter. It is also not a bad time to start making a compost heap if you don't already have one, although it probably won't get going until the weather warms up a little.

Sow under protection
Rocket, swede, cabbages, cauliflowers and celeriac.

Sow direct
Onions (from seed), broad beans, parsnips and radishes.

Crop
Cabbage, broccoli or purple sprouting, celeriac, Jerusalem artichokes, leeks, kale, parnips, radishes, rhubarb crowns (forced), rocket, spinach and Swiss chard.

Other jobs to do
- Plant rhubarb and cover with a pot to force early stalks.

- Apply organic fertilizer to the ground before sowing early crops.

- Use organic fertilizer on crops that have been growing over the winter, such as broad beans, onions and spring cabbages, as soon as you notice new growth.

- Gooseberry and currant bushes will also benefit from some organic fertilizer.

- Prune any newly planted fruit canes and bushes.

- Cut back any autumn-fruiting raspberry bushes to ground level and cover with mulch.

- If the ground is dry enough you can give it a dig to help with aeration.

- Add lime to any areas that need it, for example, the bed containing brassicas.

- Chit seed potatoes.

MARCH

Now the soil is starting to warm up your allotment will require more and more of your time. Not only will you be able to plant more, but your work will involve keeping on top of the weeds and pests that are also enjoying the spring sunshine.

Sow under protection
Aubergines, celery, celeriac, lettuces and tomatoes.

Sow direct
Broad beans, beetroot, Brussels sprouts, cabbages, carrots, cauliflowers, leeks, onions (from seed), parsnips, peas, radishes, rocket, spinach, spring onions, turnips and Swiss chard.

Plant direct
Lettuces, cauliflowers and early potatoes as soon as the ground is dry enough.

Crop
Broccoli or purple sprouting, Brussels sprouts, cabbages, cauliflowers, celeriac, Jerusalem artichokes, kale, leeks, lettuces, parsnips, radishes, rhubarb (forced), rocket, spinach and Swiss chard.

Other jobs to do
• Mulch all your soft fruits with organic matter.

• Lift and divide mint every couple of years.

• Make sure you keep on top of weeds by hoeing regularly.

• Keep a watchful eye for any slugs or other pests.

• Chit seed potatoes.

APRIL

The allotment is starting to get really busy now with everyone shrugging off the winter blues. There are plenty of jobs to do this month especially if the early part of the year has been plagued with bad weather. Start getting your plot spick and span.

Sow under protection
Aubergines, celery, celeriac, chillies, French beans, peppers, sweetcorn and tomatoes.

Sow direct
Beetroot, broad beans, broccoli or purple sprouting, Brussels sprouts, cabbage, carrots, cauliflower, chard, kale, leeks, lettuces, onions (from seed), parsnips, peas, radishes, rocket, spinach, spring onions, Swiss chard and turnips.

Plant direct
Globe and Jerusalem artichokes, onion sets, potatoes.

Crop
Asparagus, broccoli or purple sprouting, leeks, rhubarb, radishes, rocket, spinach, spring onions and Swiss chard.

Other jobs to do
• Try to keep on top of the slug population as they love to eat your young plants.

• Clear your beds of any winter vegetables and prepare the ground for new planting.

• Cover your summer brassicas and carrots with mesh to keep any flying insects off the crop.

• Liquid feed any autumn-sown garlic.

MAY

Don't be fooled by the warm days, the temperature can still drop quite low at night. Make sure any tender plants are protected until the threat of frosts has passed. If you are struggling to keep on top of the weeds you might want to consider covering an unused area of your plot with a sheet of black plastic or a mulch of straw.

Sow under protection
Aubergines, celeriac, courgettes, marrow and other squashes, chillies, cucumbers, peppers, pumpkins and other winter squashes and sweetcorn.

Sow direct
Beetroot, broccoli or purple sprouting, cabbage, carrots, cauliflower, Florence fennel, French beans, kale, lettuce, leeks, parsnips, peas, radishes, rocket, runner beans, spinach, spring onions, swedes and turnips.

Plant direct
Potatoes.

Plant out
Cabbage, cauliflower, celeriac, French beans, kale, lettuce and sweetcorn.

Crop
Asparagus, broad beans, cabbage, celeriac, Jerusalem artichokes, lettuce, peas, radishes,

rhubarb, rocket, spinach, spring onions, Swiss chard and turnips.

Other jobs to do

- Thin out rows of seedlings to give them more space.

- Prepare the ground for leeks.

- Stake your broad beans to prevent them falling over.

- Put straw under and around your strawberry plants.

- Keep up the routine of hoeing, mulching and weeding.

JUNE

June is probably the busiest month on the allotment calendar. You will be cropping your harvest on an almost daily basis. Remember, the more you pick peas and French beans, the more pods they will produce. This is also the season for soft fruits, so you should be reaping the rewards from your strawberry plants and blackcurrant canes.

Sow direct

Beetroot, carrots, courgettes, marrows and other summer squash, cucumbers, Florence fennel, French beans, lettuce, peas, pumpkins and other winter squash, radishes, rocket, runner beans, spring onions and turnips.

Plant direct

Potatoes.

Plant out

Aubergines, broccoli and purple sprouting, cabbage, cauliflower, celeriac, chillies, courgettes, marrows and other summer squash, cucumbers, kale, leeks, peppers, pumpkins and other winter squash and tomatoes.

Crop

Asparagus, beetroot, broad beans, cabbage, carrots, currants, French beans, gooseberries, lettuce, onions (from sets), peas, potatoes, radishes, raspberries, rocket, rhubarb, spinach, spring onions, strawberries, Swiss chard and turnips.

Others jobs to do

- After cropping, dry shallots and garlic naturally in the sun.

- Make sure you water regularly.

- Mulch the ground to keep on top of weeds and to retain moisture.

- Put in stakes to support your tomatoes, peas and dwarf beans.

- Tie your raspberry canes to wires.

- Cover your soft fruit with netting to keep off the birds.

JULY

This is the month you associate with constant watering and wandering up and down the allotment with a watering can in each hand. You will probably find you have a glut of produce this month, as everything seems to reach its peak at the same time.

Sow direct
Beetroot, currants, Florence fennel, lettuce, peas, radishes, Swiss chard and turnips.

Plant direct
Potatoes (for winter crop), strawberries.

Plant out
Broccoli or purple sprouting, cabbage, cauliflower, kale and leeks.

Crop
Beetroot, currants, broad beans, cabbage, carrots, celery, courgettes, marrows and other summer squash, cucumbers, French beans, garlic, globe artichokes, gooseberries, lettuce, onions (from sets and seeds), peas, potatoes, radishes, raspberries, rocket, rhubarb, runner beans, shallots, spinach, spring onions, strawberries, Swiss chard and turnips.

Other jobs to do
- Hoe regularly to keep the weeds down.

- Water regularly, particularly if it has been a prolonged dry period.

- Cut down the raspberry canes as soon as they have finished fruiting. Start to tie in this year's canes.

AUGUST

Even though you are still in the height of summer, you need to start thinking about winter vegetables now. As your beds become empty you might want to plant some green manures to stop nutrients from being leached from the soil. Alternatively put some new seedlings into the recently vacated beds.

Sow direct
Cabbage, lettuce, onions (from seed), radishes, spinach, spring onions, Swiss chard and turnips.

Plant direct
Strawberries.

Plant out

Broccoli or purple sprouting, cabbage and leeks.

Crop

Aubergines, beetroot, cabbage, cauliflower, celery, chillies, courgettes, marrows and other summer squash, cucumber, French beans, garlic, globe artichokes, lettuce, onions (from sets and seeds), peas, peppers, potatoes, pumpkins and other winter squash, radishes, rocket, runner beans, shallots, spinach, spring onions, sweetcorn, Swiss chard, tomatoes and turnips.

Other jobs to do

- Keep on top of the weeding, watering and mulching.

- Stake any tall plants to prevent them drooping to the ground.

- Pinch out the top of outdoor tomatoes when you can see 4 to 5 trusses. As the days get shorter, remove the stakes from the tomatoes and lay the plants on straw to allow the fruit to ripen.

- On dry sunny days lay the onions out to dry. If it is too wet, continue to dry them indoors.

- Prepare new strawberry beds and plant out runners.

SEPTEMBER

You need to try to harvest as much of your crops as possible before the weather starts to turn. At the end of the month pick all your tomatoes, even if they are green. If you want to finish ripening you can put them in a brown paper bag with a banana, but if this doesn't work make yourself a nice batch of green tomato chutney. If you have had a particularly good crop of a specific variety of vegetable, you might like to think about keeping some seeds for next year.

Sow direct

Lettuce, radishes, rocket and spinach.

Plant direct

Onions sets, strawberries.

Plant out

Cabbage.

Crop

Aubergines, beetroot, cabbage, carrots, cauliflower, celeriac, celery, chillies, courgettes, marrows and other summer squash, cucumber, Florence fennel, French beans, globe artichokes, leeks, lettuce, onions (from sets and seeds), peas, peppers, potatoes, pumpkins and other winter squash, raspberries, rocket, runner beans, spinach, spring onions, sweetcorn, Swiss chard, tomatoes and turnips.

Other jobs to do

- Draw soil around celeriac and leeks.

- Cut off this summer's blackberry and raspberry canes to ground level. Tie in new fruit canes.

- Order new fruit bushes for winter planting.

OCTOBER

Some gardeners start to get the winter blues around about October, as the realization dawns that the winter is on its way. There is no need to feel down, there is still plenty to do and now is the time to start putting away as much of your produce as you can to see you through the months ahead. You might feel inclined to start tidying up the plot, as there is probably a lot of debris lying around on top of the soil at this time. Insects love to use this debris to make their homes, and the gardener can never have too many beneficial insects on their side. Leaves can be gathered up and put in a frame ready to make some valuable leaf mould.

Sow under protection

Lettuces, radishes and spinach.

Sow direct

Broad beans.

Plant direct

Garlic, rhubarb crowns and onion sets.

Plant out

Cabbage.

Protect from frost

Lettuces, radishes, spinach and Swiss chard.

Crop

Beetroot, Brussels sprouts, cabbage, carrots, cauliflower, celeriac, chillies, courgettes, marrows and other summer squash, Florence fennel, leeks, lettuce, onions (from sets and seeds), parsnips, peas, peppers, potatoes, pumpkins and other winter squash, radishes, raspberries (autumn fruiting), rocket, Swiss chard, turnips.

Other jobs to do

- Store all main crop potatoes in paper sacks in a dry, dark place.

- Clear any beds where the crops are finished and fork over the ground. Clear weeds as you go.

- Buy manure, soil improver or mushroom compost to fork into the empty beds.

- Sow a winter green manure if any of your beds are going to stand empty.

- Build up earth around celery and leeks.

- Separate your rhubarb by dividing mature clumps into fist-sized pieces. Plant these 1 metre apart in soil that has been well manured.

NOVEMBER

Your visits to the allotment are probably starting to decline now, especially as the evenings are now dark. Try to stay in the habit of making regular visits to make sure everything is alright and utilize the winter months to carry out any essential repairs to your shed or greenhouse.

Sow under protection
Rocket.

Sow direct
Broad beans.

Plant direct
Currants, garlic, onion sets, raspberries and rhubarb crown.

Protect
Broad beans, lettuce, peas, radishes, spinach and Swiss chard.

Crop
Brussels sprouts, cabbages, carrots, cauliflowers, celeriac, celery, Jerusalem artichokes, kale, leeks, lettuce, parsnips, potatoes, radishes, rocket, spinach, swedes, Swiss chard and turnips.

Other jobs to do
- This is a good month for digging before the weather turns really cold or wet.

- Dig in well-rotted manure or compost where the peas, beans, onions and leeks, celery and spinach are to be planted next year.

- Now is the time to cut your globe artichoke (*left*) stems to ground level. Cover with soil to protect them.

- Lift mint roots and divide up into smaller plots that can be placed on a sunny windowsill and used over the winter.

DECEMBER

Now is the time to sit back and take stock of what you have achieved over the last year. Remember the day when you first took over the plot at the allotment and how daunting the task seemed? Well you did it – you survived a year and had several successes and failures, no doubt. If the weather is really bad, you can sit down and sketch a plan of what you would like to grow next year, keeping in mind the crop rotation scheme. You can use some of your crops over the Christmas festivities, such as onions to make some delicious stuffing or some of your potatoes and parsnips for the roasties. You won't need to fight in the supermarket, either, for the last few Brussels sprouts, you can pick them straight off the plant into your pan. It might even encourage some of your dinner guests to think about taking an allotment as well.

Sow under protection
Rocket.

Plant direct
Currants, garlic, raspberries and shallots.

Protect
Lettuce, spinach and Swiss chard.

Crop
Brussels sprouts, cabbages, cauliflowers, celeriac, Jerusalem artichokes, kale, leeks, lettuce, parsnips, radishes, rocket, spinach, swedes, Swiss chard and turnips.

Other jobs to do
• Protect bay, rosemary and oregano with fleece if the weather turns really cold.

• Ask other people on the allotment whether they would like to share a load of well-rotted manure.

• Make sure all your notes are up to date, including your failures as well as your successes.

YUMMY CHRISTMAS STUFFING
This stuffing is also great in turkey sandwiches for the Christmas supper.

Ingredients
225 g sausage meat
225 g smoked streaky bacon
225 g onion, chopped
225 g cooked chestnuts
150 g dried cranberries
100 g breadcrumbs
1 egg

Method
1. Snip the bacon into small pieces and fry until it is crisp. Fry the onion until it is soft and flavoured with the bacon fat.

2. Mix the rest of the ingredients together, bind with the egg and either stuff the turkey or eat separately as stuffing balls.

COMPANION PLANTING

Although this doesn't strictly come under the heading of A Gardener's Calendar, the gardener needs to be aware of the importance of companion planting. When planning your site you need to make room for a few rows of flowers, which are traditionally grown as companion plants. You have probably already seen rows of marigolds mingled in with rows of vegetables and there is a reason for this. By planting certain plants close to vegetables, you are not only deterring pests and diseases, but you are increasing the flavour and yield of your crop. Some of these companion plants are so attractive to pests, that you might find they leave your crop alone completely. The strong odours of leeks, chives and garlic planted next to a row of carrots, works well to confuse the carrot fly. Although there is no set rule as to the best companions, the following list is designed to give you a guidelines as to the ones that work most successfully.

FRENCH MARIGOLD (*Tagetes patula*)
This plant helps to repel soil nematodes and whitefly from tomatoes and are good companions to most plants. They should be spaced 25 to 30 cm apart in rows between the plants.

CALIFORNIAN POPPY (*Eschscholzia californica*)
This is a good aphid repellant that has pretty orange flowers with bluish-green leaves. It should be sown in early summer directly into the ground and thinned to 20 cm apart.

MORNING GLORY (*Ipomoea tricolor*)
This is traditionally used as a companion plant, as it tends to attract hoverflies. It has bright blue, trumpet-shaped flowers and can be sown directly into the grown, thinning to 20 cm.

NASTURTIUM (*Nasturtium tropaeolum*)
Wherever you see beans you tend to find nasturtiums, as they are great at deterring blackfly. So that you do not lose the nasturtium totally to blackfly, plant a row of marigolds alongside to attract the hoverflies that love to eat aphids. Sow in mid-spring directly into the ground, one seed to every 16 cm.

POACHED EGG PLANT (*Limnanthes douglassi*)
These are low-growing plants with pretty yellow and white flowers. These attract hoverflies and will self-seed freely. Sow directly in the ground in late spring, 15 to 20 cm apart.

In addition to these flowers, all herbs work especially well as companion plants. They are able to attract beneficial insects while repelling pests, so should be planted freely.

What to Grow

CHOOSE YOUR CROPS

Once you have acquired an allotment or space for growing vegetables you need to plan your plot and choose the types of plants. For good reason the vast majority of plants grown on allotments are vegetables but there is no reason why you should not be more adventurous.

You only need to pick up any good seed catalogue to realize there is a huge choice of plants to grow. There is a number of things to bear in mind when choosing which plants will be worth growing.

The most important factor in choosing crops is the suitability of the soil and site and your family favourites. For example, there is no advantage in growing rows of Brussels sprouts if no one in your family actually likes them.

This section is a guide to the requirements of crops that can be grown on allotments given the right conditions. Don't be disappointed if you have a few failures in the first year, as this could be down to the condition of the soil and the fact that it hasn't yet benefitted from the extra nutrients. It could be that it wasn't warm enough when you planted out, or the crop was plagued by pests. Whatever the reason, do not be disheartened; try again next year and you will probably find you have a very different outcome.

There are many varieties to choose from and at first the choice might be a bit confusing, but trial and error is the key here. Many of the more modern strains have been developed to produce hardy, more uniform vegetables, particularly for the commercial market. This means that many of the old heritage plants are dying out and can be difficult to find. However, if you are able to find the older varieties you will find the flavours are far superior and the unusual shapes make them fun to grow.

If you don't want to start with seeds – and there is no shame in this because young seedlings are much more reliable – plug plants are ideal. To bring on seeds you will either need sunny windowsills or a warm greenhouse and endless seed trays, but you might like to try a few when you first get your allotment. Some plants, particularly salad crops and brassicas, benefit from being started off in a controlled environment, which means they can get going without the threat of slug or snail damage.

ROOT & STEM CROPS

Root crops

Root crops could be seen as the unsung heroes of the vegetable garden. Maybe it is because a root crop is out of sight while building up its energy store of sugars and starches. When it is dug up it is often not as handsome as any other vegetable. Some roots, such as parsnips for example, have a strong flavour that many people dislike. Then there are crops such as potatoes and carrots that are loved by nearly everyone. Nevertheless root crops should take prominence in your vegetable patch because they can be easy to grow, are tasty and some types can even be a little exotic. Although mainly associated with providing warming, filling food during the colder months, they also provide the joy of new potatoes, baby carrots, radishes and beetroot in the summer.

All root crops do better in a well prepared, deeply dug soil. A sandy, fine loam, free from stones and lumps is the ideal soil for root vegetables. Heavy soils in particular benefit from the addition of horticultural sand. All types of root crops benefit from a soil high in organic matter and this should be dug into the soil in the autumn before cropping.

Stem crops

Celery, celeriac (*right*), Florence fennel and kohl rabi are the main stem crops. Rhubarb is listed elsewhere because it is grown on a permanent plot and has slightly different requirements.

Crop rotation

Potatoes, should go on soil that has been freshly manured following on from brassicas. Other root vegetables can follow on from peas and beans, as they do not like soil that has been freshly disturbed, so following potatoes is not a good idea.

Some plants used for their roots are from the Brassica family (for example, turnips and swedes) and must not be planted before or following on from other brassicas.

Avoid having beetroot planted before or following Swiss chard or spinach.

Carrots, celery, parsnip and parsley should not follow on from each other.

POTATOES

Solanum tuberosum

QUICK REFERENCE

Soil

Deeply dug soil with a high organic-matter content. Scab can be a problem in alkaline soils. pH 5 to 6.5 is ideal.

Position

Open, sunny position free from danger of frost.

Planting time

Early varieties, early to mid-spring. Main crops, mid to late spring.

Spacing

30 to 36 cm apart with 30 to 45 cm between rows for earlies and 75 to 90 cm between rows for main crops.

Pests and diseases

Eelworm, slugs and blight.

Quick tips

Potatoes can grow well in large containers.

The cultivation of potatoes on newly acquired plots prepares the ground well for other types of vegetables, making them an ideal 'pioneer' crop.

EARLIES AND MAIN CROPS

Potato are classified as first earlies, second earlies or main crop according to what time of year they crop. Frost is a big enemy, so you need to keep an eye on the weather.

Depending on weather conditions first and second earlies can be planted in the south of the UK in mid-March; in the north by late March/early April.

First earlies should be ready for lifting 10 weeks after planting and second earlies, 13 weeks after planting.

Main-crop potatoes can be planted in the south during the first half of April and further north by late April. They should be ready to lift 15 to 20 weeks after planting.

Many gardeners choose only to grow early potatoes. There are a few reasons for this. When main-crop potatoes are ready for harvest, potatoes are usually readily and cheaply available in the shops. Main-crop potatoes take up a lot of space and time at a point when there are more valuable crops to grow. Blight is a problem for main crops but does not usually affect earlies.

BEST VARIETIES

Only use seed tubers that are certified free from disease.

First earlies

'Red Duke of York' is one of the earliest to

crop, has a pale yellow flesh with a sweet flavour and is good for baking.

'International Kidney' is an outstanding salad potato (known as 'Jersey Royal' when it is grown in Jersey).

'Belle de Fontenay' is a favourite of the French, used boiled or in salads.

'Epicure' has a distinctive flavour, used boiled or baked.

Second earlies
'Charlotte' is good boiled and excellent cold in salads.

'Kestrel' has some resistance to slugs and is good for all dishes except salads.

Main crop
'Pink Fir Apple' is an old variety with an excellent nutty flavour, so good that if you grow only one main crop, this should be it.

'Sarpo Mira' has good resistance to blight and slugs and is good, boiled or roasted.

SOIL
Potatoes grow reasonably well in most soils, but the best results are obtained from land that has been deeply dug and well manured in the previous autumn.

CHITTING
Chitting is the process of encouraging seed potatoes to put out strong healthy shoots before planting.

Put the seed potatoes in a cool, frost-free location where they receive some light but not direct sunlight. A north-facing window is ideal. The potatoes will then start to grow short stubby chits (shoots). Allow only two or three chits to grow on each seed potato; rub any extra ones off with your thumb.

PLANTING
Wilted comfrey leaves can be placed at the bottom of the planting hole, under the seed potato and covered with a little soil. This acts as a fertilizer.

Plant early potatoes about 10 cm deep and mains 20 cm deep. Pop the seed potato in, chits up and pull the soil from the sides to cover.

Plant early potatoes about 30 cm apart in rows about 45 cm apart. Main-crop potatoes should be 30 to 36 cm apart in rows 75 to 90 cm apart.

EARTHING UP
As the plants start to grow, rake earth from the sides of the rows to form a ridge along the top of the plants. This will prevent light reaching the tubers which will turn them green and inedible. The earthing-up process also removes many weeds.

FEEDING
A fortnight before planting apply a general fertilizer at 60–90g per square metre.

WATERING

If you do water, be sure to drench the soil. Water earlies during very dry spells. Do not water main crops until the tubers are at least marble sized.

PESTS AND DISEASES

Blight can strike in hot and humid conditions and causes the potatoes to rot. The first symptoms are dark blotches on the leaves. If you see this act quickly: cut down and remove all of the foliage and you may prevent the blight reaching the tubers. Leave the crop in the ground for 2 to 3 weeks before lifting.

Blight is usually a problem for main-crop potatoes, as it generally strikes late in the season; this is one reason why many vegetable gardeners choose to grow only earlies.

Scab affects plants grown in alkaline conditions. The tubers are still edible if the scabby patches are cut away. Resistant cultivars are available. Test your soil and if necessary adjust it to pH 5 to 6.5 before planting.

PLANTING IN CONTAINERS

Growing potatoes in containers is easy and there are advantages to doing so. There is no heavy digging and earthing up. The potatoes are planted in multi-purpose compost and therefore the risk of pests or disease is very low. Containers can be protected from frost by placing them in a greenhouse or under fleece. Growing in containers can extend the growing season; it is even possible to crop potatoes at Christmas.

Ideally the container should be at least 50 cm in diameter and 50 cm tall to take 4 to 6 seed potatoes. For one seed potato, a 25 cm diameter and 25 cm tall pot will do. Make sure the container has drainage holes. Half fill the pot with compost and bury the seed potatoes just below the surface. As the shoots grow, cover them with compost until the pot is full; this serves the same purpose as 'earthing up'. Water regularly, keeping the compost moist but not water logged. Feed with a general-purpose fertilizer if the leaves turn yellow. In June you can start testing the size of the tubers by putting your hand into the compost and taking some as new potatoes if you wish. Be sure to keep all tubers well covered with compost.

Potatoes can be grown in sacks or plastic bin bags. Roll down the top half of the bag, put multi-purpose compost in the bag to a depth of 10 to 15 cm and plant a chitted seed potato. The plastic bag can be put wherever it's convenient, as long as it's not too shady. Punch holes in the bottom of the bag for drainage.

For potatoes late in the year, hold back some of your seed potatoes from the main season, wrap them individually in newspaper, then put them all in a paper bag and keep them in a cold store or refrigerator. Around the end of August, take them out of the cold store/refrigerator and go through the chitting process. Plant containers with chitted early potato tubers from September onwards in a cool greenhouse protected from the frost. The plants will produce crops from early December through the winter.

NO-DIG POTATOES

Potatoes can be planted on the surface of the soil and mulched with straw. Growing in straw is an old Northern European way of growing potatoes. This no-dig method is easy and will yield a good crop; it is a good way to get a newly acquired plot to produce crops quickly. Prepare the site in spring by clearing any surface weeds with a mower or brush cutter. Cover the soil with a 5 cm layer of manure and dampen it. Cover the manure with cardboard or a thick layer of wet newspaper, overlapping the sheets to ensure there are no gaps. When all risk of frost has passed, put the seed potatoes on the newspaper 50 cm apart and cover with a 10-cm layer of straw. Add a 5-cm layer of manure over the straw. As the potato shoots appear above the manure, add another layer of staw and manure and repeat as neccesary.

HARVESTING

Lift early potatoes as and when you need them, as they are better when freshly dug. You can harvest 'new' potatoes by gently scraping back the soil and taking a few from each plant and leaving the rest in the ground until needed. Be sure to remove all potatoes from the ground; any left may harbour disease and pests.

Main crops should be lifted when the foliage dies back.

STORING

Use new potatoes as soon as possible. Before storing main-crop potatoes, they should be left out in the sun for a few hours to dry off and allow the skins to harden a little. Excess soil should be brushed off and they should not be washed. Check for and remove any damaged tubers before storing in paper sacks in a dark place at around 5 to 10°C. Leave the bags slightly open to allow moisture to escape. Check them regularly for any signs of rot or slugs.

CARROTS

Daucus carota

QUICK REFERENCE

Soil
Light, fine soil, not recently been manured and is free from lumps or stones. Plant cylinder and globe-shape carrots if your soil is shallow. pH of 6.5 to 7.5 is preferred.

Position
Unfussy about site but early varieties of carrot do best in full sun; main crops prefer some shade.

Planting time
Can be sown under protection of cloches in early spring and through to July for cropping in October.

Spacing
Sow thinly, 1 to 2 cm deep and thin to 10 cm. Space rows 15cm apart.

Pests and diseases
Carrot fly, splitting and violet root rot.

Quick tip
By interplanting carrots and onions you can confuse and help to deter both carrot and onion fly.

BEST VARIETIES
'Nantes' and 'Chantenay' are reliable and quick growing for early in the season.

'Autumn King' is good for late-season harvesting and stores well.

'Parmex' and 'Parabel' are round-rooted and good for growing in containers and heavy or shallow soils.

SOIL
Carrots prefer a light soil free from stones that has been dug to a spade's depth and had a fine tilth created. Carrots grown on heavy soil or where organic material has recently been applied will become misshapen and grow forked. Sandy soil can be improved with well-rotted compost dug in two to three months before sowing to improve water retention.

If you have heavy and/or shallow soil, they are an ideal vegetable to be grown in raised beds. Do not plant in soil that may become waterlogged.

SOWING
Carrots can be sown over quite a long period so that they are ready for eating from early June to October.

Sown under the protection of cloches, early varieties such as 'Early Nantes' and

'Amsterdam', can be harvested as early as June. Main-crop carrots can be planted through to late summer.

Run a trowel along a wooden plank to produce a drill 2 cm deep; position the drills 12 cm apart. Drop a couple of seeds every 2 cm along the drills. Sow the seed thinly to avoid too much thinning out later. Cover the seeds with fine soil and water with a fine spray. The seedlings should start showing about 15 to 20 days later.

THINNING

Remember to thin carrot seedlings out to avoid overcrowding as soon as the seedlings are about 2.5 cm high. Thin early varieties to about 13 cm apart and main-crop varieties to 20 cm apart. Be aware that thinning out can entice carrot fly, as they will be attracted by the smell, so try and do it in the evening when this pest is not active.

FEEDING

Fork in a handful of bonemeal for each square metre at least 2 weeks before planting. Do not feed while the plants are growing.

WATERING

The crop is better when well watered. Water regularly in dry weather but do not allow to become waterlogged.

PESTS AND DISEASES

Carrot have only one major problem: the carrot fly. This black fly is about 1 cm long and lays its eggs in loose soil around the carrot. These eggs mature into yellow maggots, which then attack the carrots, causing serious damage. Leaf discolouration and tunnels in the carrot are the signs to look for.

The flies are most common in mid-May, so holding back on sowing main-crop varieties till June can be a good idea. Be aware, the carrot fly may also be attracted by parsley, celery, parsnip and celeriac.

Carrot flies do not fly higher than around 50 to 60 cm, so a barrier/fence all around the crop, made of plastic or fleece, 1 metre high, should keep them away. Another barrier method is to use enviromesh laid on top of the crop.

Interplant onions with carrots, as the smells may help deter both carrot and onion fly.

HARVESTING

Carrots that are harvested before full maturity will be tender and tastier than those left in the ground.

STORING

If you have a bumper crop, they can be stored in a box of slightly moist peat or sand and placed in a cool, frost-free, dark place. Stored in this way they should keep for a couple of months.

BEETROOT

Beta vulgaris

QUICK REFERENCE

Soil

Light, well drained, fine soil that has not recently been manured. pH of 6.5 to 7.5 is ideal.

Position

Unfussy but does best in a sunny position.

Planting time

Mid-spring to mid-summer for most varieties. Sowings in early spring should be of a type resistant to bolting.

Spacing

Sow thinly, in rows 30 cm apart and thin to 15 cm apart.

Pests and diseases

Very few pests and diseases attack beetroot, almost trouble free.

Quick tips

Remember the leaves are edible too! Use the leaves in the same way you would use Swiss chard.

Golden beetroot is as good if not better than the red varieties.

Beetroot is an ideal crop. It is very versatile as a food, providing leaves and young beets for salads, then bigger beets suitable for boiling or roasting in autumn dishes.

It is very easy to grow, suffering from few problems. The major fault to afflict beetroot is bolting (running to seed); this may occur during an extended cold spell when temperatures are below 10°C for more than two weeks. If a long, cold spell is predicted cover the crop with cloches or fleece.

SOIL

Beetroot is best grown on medium to light, free-draining soil. Dig the soil deeply, removing as many stones as possible. Add manure or compost to the soil in the season before growing beetroot.

BEST VARIETIES

'Boltardy' is bolt resistant and good for early sowings. Deep red, medium-sized, globe-shaped roots.

'Burpee's Golden' is a delicious, sweet-tasting, golden root that also provides greens for salad or cooking.

'Choggia' reveals concentric rings of pink and white when sliced but is not merely a novelty because the roots are sweet and the greens can be used like spinach.

'Red Ace' is a good reliable main crop.

'Pablo' is a fast-growing, miniature root with good flavour.

SOWING

Beetroot should not be sowed outside until after the last frost. Sowing can be brought forward a few weeks if you use a polytunnel or cloche or sow in modules indoors. Use bolt-resistant varieties for early sowings. Sow a small amount every three weeks from spring to mid-summer for a continuous crop.

Soak beetroot seeds for a few hours before sowing. If sowing in rows leave around 30 cm between rows. Sow at around 2 cm depth, 5 cm apart and cover with soil. After sowing make sure the soil remains damp until the seeds have germinated and you can see the emerging seedlings.

THINNING

Each seed cluster actually contains one to four seeds. When the seedlings emerge there may be more than one from each seed cluster; snip off all but the strongest with small scissors. After the seedlings have reached about 5 cm in height you can thin them to about 10 cm apart.

FEEDING

Beetroot does not require fertilizer but a spray with a seaweed-based, foliar fertilizer would supply trace elements.

WATERING

Water in hot, dry periods. Keep the soil moist and give the roots a good drenching when they start to swell.

PESTS AND DISEASES

Birds may pull up young seedlings. Deter them with bird scarers.

HARVESTING

Should be available July to October if sown successively from May to July. Harvest globe varieties when between 5 and 8 cm in diameter, as any further growth will make them woody and less palatable.

Harvest by pulling up the roots and twisting off the greens.

STORING

Brush off any loose soil but do not wash the roots; try not to damage the roots or they will bleed. Beetroot greens can be stored in the refrigerator for up to 10 days. Keep the roots in the refrigerator for up to 20 days.

For long-term storage put the beetroot in boxes separated by sand in a cool, dark and frost-free place.

Roots can be left in the ground until needed if protected by a layer of straw, 15 cm thick.

Don't forget that pickling is a good way to keep beetroot and a good way to benefit from a glut.

RADISHES

Raphanus sativus

QUICK REFERENCE

Soil
Fertile and moisture-retentive soil with a pH of 5.5 to 7 is ideal but radishes tolerate most soil types as long as it has not recently been manured.

Position
An open site is preferred but radishes do better with some light shade in hot, sunny conditions.

Planting time
Sow small quantities of summer radish in early spring and all through summer. Sow winter radish in late summer.

Spacing
Sow summer radish, 2.5 cm apart in rows 15 cm apart. Sow winter radish, 20 cm apart in rows 30 cm apart.

Pests and diseases
Flea beetles and cabbage root fly.

Quick tips
Radishes are an ideal crop to fit in around others wherever there is space because they are so quick to mature.

Radishes are an ideal vegetable for the novice gardener, as they are easy to grow.

Sow winter radishes from mid-summer onwards; they are bigger than summer varieties and can be eaten hot or cold.

BEST VARIETIES

Summer varieties
'French Breakfast' has a crisp, mild flavour.

'Scarlet Globe' is popular and fast growing.

'Short Top Forcing' is good for growing in cold frames or cloches.

'Champion' is very easy to grow, medium-sized and crunchy.

'Hong Vit' is grown for baby roots but mainly for leaves. Cultivate like cress or mustard for hairless leaves with pink stems and a mild radish flavour. Harvest as baby leaves, baby veg or full-sized bunched leaves for soups, salads or stir fries.

Winter varieties
'Mino Early' is a winter variety that can be eaten hot or cold.

'Black Spanish Round' has black skin but white and succulent flesh.

SOIL

A well-dug soil with a fine tilth and no stones or fresh compost in it is ideal. Add a handful of bonemeal one month before sowing. Organic matter added months before sowing will help retain moisture.

SOWING

Sow summer radish seed little but often to ensure a continuous supply.

For summer varieties start sowing in mid-April and continue at two-week intervals into September. Sow thinly, 5 mm deep and in drills 15 cm apart.

If radishes are grown in full sun during the summer, they will run to seed or bolt very quickly. For this reason, grow them where they will benefit from the shade of other plants such as peas and beans.

Sow winter varieties from mid-summer through to late autumn. Sowing winter radish too early can result in bolting.

Sow the larger-rooted winter varieties in drills 30 cm apart.

THINNING

Thin out any overcrowded plants when they are large enough. Thin summer radish to 2.5 cm apart and winter radish to 15 cm apart.

FEEDING

Feed the soil with a handful of bonemeal one month before sowing.

WATERING

Water regularly but do not overwater; too much water will produce green growth at the expense of root growth.

PESTS AND DISEASES

Radishes are part of the brassica family and therefore can be attacked by flea beetle; generally this only affects the leaves. Do not plant in ground where club root is a problem.

Take precautions against slugs, especially with the winter radishes, which stay in the ground longer.

HARVESTING

Pull summer radishes as soon as they are large enough (2.5 cm in diameter); they become 'pithy' and the roots will split if left too long.

Winter radish can be left in the ground until needed, although they may be damaged by frost or slugs.

If some of your plants bolt and run to seed, the pods, if harvested while still green and crisp, are tasty additions to salads. The seeds can be sprouted like cress, and yield nutritious young shoots for salads.

STORING

Store summer radishes in the refrigerator until needed. Winter radishes can be stored packed loosely in sand in a box and kept in a cool, frost-free, dark place.

PARSNIPS

Pastinaca sativa

QUICK REFERENCE

Soil
Deep, stone-free soil. pH 6 to 7.

Position
Open, sunny site.

Planting time
Can be sown any time from late winter to late spring.

Spacing
Sow seeds 10 to 20 cm apart, in rows 30 cm apart.

Pests and diseases
Wireworm, sclerotina rot, canker, leaf spot, celery fly, carrot fly.

Quick tips
Parsnip seed can be hard to germinate. To increase your success, make sure your seed is fresh, as it deteriorates quickly.

Seed sown in spring is more likely to germinate than that sown in late winter.

There are short-rooted varieties of parsnip available that are more suited to be grown in shallow soils.

Parsnips are very easy to grow. The main problem with them is the amount of time they take to mature, which means they may occupy the space on your allotment for almost the full year.

BEST VARIETIES

'Gladiator' is canker resistant and able to grow large without becoming woody.

'Tender and True' is reliable with excellent flavour.

'Avonresister' has good disease resistance, good flavour and fairly short roots, making it more suitable for shallow soils.

'Lancer' and 'Arrow' are both varieties that are suitable for sowing more densely and cropping young and small.

SOIL

Parsnips are best grown in ground that was manured well for a previous crop. Freshly manured ground is likely to cause the roots to fork. Avoid stony ground as the parsnip roots will be deflected and the parsnips will become misshapen.

In late autumn dig the ground deeply, removing stones, then leave rough until sowing time. Just before sowing, break the soil down to a fine tilth.

SOWING TIMES

The traditional time to sow parsnip seed is late winter, but germination rates are usually more successful if seed is sown in early spring.

SOWING

Make the drills for parsnips 2.5 cm deep and 30 cm apart. Sow three or four seeds together then lightly rake the soil over the drills to cover the seeds.

THINNING

When the seedlings are about 5 cm tall, thin them out to 20 cm apart.

FEEDING

No special feeding requirements.

WATERING

Water well during the early stages and be careful not to damage the roots when weeding. Do not let the soil dry out.

PESTS AND DISEASES

Parsnip canker may be a problem if parsnips are grown in wet, acid soils. The symptoms are brown sunken areas on the top of the roots. The canker can be cut away and the root can be used straight away; do not store affected roots. To prevent canker, make sure the soil is free draining, test the pH and lime if neccessary.

Carrot flies are small black flies 1 cm long that may be present in mid-May. The maggots may tunnel in to parsnip roots.

Protect the crop by covering it with enviromesh in May.

Keep you parsnips well weeded to help prevent wireworm.

HARVESTING

Lift a few roots in November in case the ground becomes frozen. You can leave most of the roots in the ground and lift as needed. Frost causes parsnips to become sweeter because it converts starches into sugars. If you still have some roots in the ground in February harvest them and store.

A problem with harvesting parsnips is that the roots are quite fragile and break. To make it easier, first dig a trench along the side of the parsnips, then scrape away the soil from the root with a trowel.

STORING

Cut the tops off and lay the roots on a bed of dry sand in a suitable box, then cover the layers of parsnips with more sand. Store boxes in a dry well-ventilated, dark place.

TURNIPS

Brassica rapa

Turnips are very easy to grow, tasty and nutritious.

BEST VARIETIES

'Purple Top Milan' is a good early variety.

'Snowball' is a fast-growing early variety that can be sown from early spring to late autumn.

SOIL

Turnips do better in a light/medium soil free from stones that is rich in organic matter, having been manured for a previous crop. pH 6 to 7.

POSITION

Will grow in full sun or light shade.

SOWING TIMES

Turnips can be sown from early spring to late summer. The seeds will germinate in soil temperatures as low as 4°C, and do better in cool weather.

SOWING

Sow the seeds thinly in drills 1 cm deep, with 38 cm between the rows.

THINNING

Thin the seedlings as soon as they are large enough to handle, to about 7 cm apart.

FEEDING

Turnips are light feeders and have no special requirements for fertilizer.

WATERING

Keep the soil well watered or the turnips may bolt and the roots will become stringy.

PESTS AND DISEASES

Turnips are more often affected by disease than they are by pests.

As they are a brassica, club root can be a problem. Avoid this by using crop rotation and do not plant on the same spot in which brassicas have just been grown. Do not let the soil get too acidic. Check the pH level and make sure it stays above 6.

To prevent problems with root maggots, flea beetles and aphids, cover the plant with enviromesh in the early part of the season.

HARVESTING

Don't allow turnips to get bigger than 4 to 6 cm in diameter. Large turnips tend to be stringy and will have strong flavour.

Harvest turnip tops sparingly from each plant while they are young and use as greens.

STORING

Turnips will keep for three to four months in a dark, cool, frost-free place.

SWEDES

Brassica napus napobrassica

Swedes are well-suited to allotment growing. They crop for a long time and can be left in the soil throughout the winter.

BEST VARIETIES
'Willemsburger' is resistant to club root and keeps well.

'Marian' is resistant to club root and mildew.

'Invitation' is hardy and also has good disease resistance.

SOIL
Swedes do better in a medium soil with a good supply of nutrients. Add some well-rotted manure or bonemeal at least one month before sowing seed.

The soil should not be too acidic, pH 6.5 to 7.5 is ideal. Lime if necessary.

If the soil is prone to waterlogging in winter, grow them on a ridge.

POSITION
Will grow in full sun or light shade.

SOWING TIMES
Early spring until early summer.

SOWING
Form a drill about 3 cm deep and sow thinly. If you are sowing more than one row then the rows should be 60 cm apart.

THINNING
Thin seedlings out to about 25 cm apart when large enough to handle.

FEEDING
No special feeding requirements.

WATERING
Water regularly in hot, dry conditions or you will have woody, strong-tasting roots.

PESTS AND DISEASES
Drooping leaves and distorted roots are indications of club root; use the same precautions as listed for turnips.

Watch out for slugs, wireworms, aphids and flea beetles.

HARVESTING
Harvest roots when 4 to 6 cm in diameter.

Don't forget swedes are members of the brassica family and this means the leaves are good for eating. It is important that you pick no more than half the leaves of each plant to cook as greens.

STORING
Twist off the leaves and store the roots in a box of sand.

SALSIFY

Tragopogon porrifolius

Salsify resembles a pale, slender parsnip and has a delicate flavour said to be reminiscent of oysters. Very deserving of a spot in the allotment because it is so easy to grow. Be sure to use only fresh seed.

BEST VARIETIES
'Sandwich Island' has an excellent flavour and smooth texture.

SOIL
Salsify grows best in light loam, well prepared to a fine tilth and raked to a level surface. Grow in a plot in which the soil was well manured for a previous crop, as fresh manure or compost must not be incorporated in the soil before planting.

A handful of general fertilizer can be raked into the surface when preparing the ground in early April.

POSITION
Prefers an open but not exposed position.

SOWING TIMES
Early to mid-spring.

SOWING
Sow salsify in drills 12 mm deep during late April or early May, sowing three seeds together. Allow 15 cm between each batch of seeds.

THINNING
After germination thin out to leave just one strong plant per station.

CULTIVATION
Water well during periods of dry weather. Water the soil and not the foliage to reduce the risk of white blister.

Keep the crop clear of weeds, being careful not to damage the crowns.

PESTS AND DISEASES
Generally free of pests but can suffer with white blister. The symptoms of white blister are chalky, white blisters on the underside of the leaves. This is a fungal disease that can be prevented by not overcrowding.

HARVESTING
Salsify can be lifted in the autumn for storing, but the roots are hardy and can be left in the ground and lifted as required. Be careful when harvesting, as the roots break easily.

If you leave roots in the ground, mulch with straw in very cold areas. In spring the tender shoots make an appetizing green vegetable and the flower buds are edible when fried in butter.

STORING
Store in boxes of sand kept cool and dark.

SCORZONERA

Scorzonera hispanica

Scorzonera is similar to Salsify but has black skin over a pure white root. The roots should be cleaned but not peeled then boiled for about 10 minutes. The outer skin can then be peeled off. They can then be roasted like pasnips.

BEST VARIETIES

'Black Giant of Russia' is the easiest seed to find and also the most reliable.

'Habil' is easy to grow and very tasty.

SOIL

Scorzonera should be planted in light, deep, stone-free soil. pH 6.5 to 7.5.

POSITION

Scorzonera prefers an open, sunny position.

SOWING TIMES

Sow as soon as the soil is warming up in early spring. The seeds need to be fresh for reliable germination.

SOWING

Sow seeds thinly in drills 12 mm deep and allowing 35 mm between rows.

THINNING

Thin the seedlings in two or more stages until they are 20 to 35 cm apart.

CULTIVATION

Water in dry weather to keep the soil moist, then mulch.

PESTS AND DISEASES

Generally trouble free.

HARVESTING

Harvest in autumn for storing or leave in the ground, protected by a straw mulch and lift as required.

Harvest the roots carefully, as they are fragile and will bleed if they break. Dig a trench alongside the row and take the soil away from the roots with a trowel.

If the roots are small they can be left in the ground for a second season to bulk up. Young shoots in spring can be eaten like asparagus and the flowers can be used in salads.

STORING

Store in boxes of damp sand, kept in a cool, dark place.

SWEET POTATO

Ipomoea batatas

Sweet potatoes first came to Europe in the 15th century. Henry VIII was said to be very fond of them and he allegedly challenged any gardener to grow them successfully in England. Despite their best efforts no one succeeded. Today sweet potatoes can be grown in the UK, given the right conditions.

BEST VARIETIES

'T65' has been bred to suit being grown in cooler conditions.

SOIL

A slightly acid, highly fertile, free-draining soil is required.

POSITION

Sweet potatoes need to be grown in temperatures of 22 to 28°C and do better in humid conditions. They can be grown outside in warmer parts of the UK in sheltered, sunny sites but will be more succesfully grown under cover in polytunnels or greenhouses.

SLIPS

Sweet potatoes are grown from sprouted shoots or 'slips'. Obtain and start growing slips in late February/early March. Slips can be ordered from seed company websites or you can grow your own from tubers from supermarkets. The disadvantage of supermarket tubers is that you probably won't have a variety bred for growing in cooler climates. Supermarket tubers may be treated with an anti-sprouting agent, so scrub them well to remove this. Place the tubers in moist sand and keep warm. The slips will emerge from the surface. When they are more than 10cm long, gently twist them off and pot into 1-litre pots and allow to grow on.

PLANTING

Plant in late May when all risk of frost has passed. If growing outside, form a ridge to plant into and warm the soil by covering it with black plastic for several weeks before planting. Plant 5 to 8 cm deep, with 30 cm between plants and 70 cm between ridges.

ROUTINE CARE

Water regularly and feed with a general-purpose fertilizer every two weeks until the tubers have formed.

HARVESTING

Carefully dig them up in late September. Once dug, sweet potatoes need to be cured: leave them to mature for two weeks in a warm area, ideally a humid 25°C. This enables the skins to set, heals wounds and improves the flavour by allowing starches to convert to sugar.

FLORENCE FENNEL

Foeniculum vulgare var. azoricum

While fennel is grown for its leaves and seeds, Florence fennel bulks up at the base of the stem to produce aromatic bulbs. The plants are handsome and decorative and, even more important, also attract beneficial insects.

BEST VARIETIES

'Romanesco' is reliable, resistant to bolting and delicious.

'Victorio' is a reliable and fast grower, suitable for late sowings.

'Zefa Fino' is bolt resistant and fast growing.

SOIL

Fennel thrives in a fertile, well-drained soil that has been manured for a previous crop.

POSITION

A sheltered position in full sun is prefered.

SOWING TIMES

Sow indoors in modules in mid-spring or sow outside in position in early summer. Bolt-resistant varieties can be sown as early as February.

SOWING/PLANTING

Sow outside 1 cm deep, spaced 30 cm apart. Plant young plants 30 cm apart.

ROUTINE CARE

Feeding should not be required. Keep the plants well-watered; if they do not get enough water they will bolt. Mulch to conserve water. Hoe regularly to keep free of weeds. Earth up the stem bases when they start to swell, this will support the plants and blanch the stems, making them sweeter.

Elongating bulbs indicate that the plant is about to run to seed. Harvest these quickly and they will still be usable.

PESTS AND DISEASES

Fennel is rarely affected by pest or disease.

HARVESTING

Harvest when about the size of a tennis ball. This can be as early as June and go through to November if you have staggered sowings. If you cut them at ground level leaving a stump; this will re-grow producing shoots for salads. The leaves can also be harvested sparingly while the stems are bulking up.

STORING

Florence fennel is best eaten as freshly as possible but can be stored in a plastic container in the refrigerator for several days. The bulbs can be frozen if trimmed, cut into slices and blanched for 3 minutes. Place in the freezer in plastic bags.

CELERY

Apium graveolens

QUICK REFERENCE

Soil
Prefers a deep, humus-rich and water-retentive soil. pH 6.8 is the ideal.

Position
Warm and sheltered, sunny site.

Sowing time
Early spring.

Spacing
Self blanching: 23 cm between plants in rows 23 cm apart.
Trench: 30 to 40 cm between plants in rows 30 cm apart.

Pests and diseases
Carrot fly, celery fly, slugs and snails, bolting, leaf spot, heart rot.

Celery is probably one of the more difficult crops to grow on an allotment, as it needs a lot of time and attention. There are three main types of celery: leaf celery, trench celery and self-blanching celery. Leaf celery is a small plant that can be grown in containers for salad leaves.

Trench celery needs a lot of space and time and more than a little skill to grow well. Traditionally growing trench celery involves planting the seedlings at the bottom of a trench and filling in the trench as they grow. This blanches the stems and makes them grow longer. Most trench celery is now grown on level ground and the stems are blanched by using collars of black plastic, loosely tied around the plants when 23 cm tall.

Self-blanching celery has off-white stalks and is a lot simpler to grow than trench celery, although not as hardy. Self-blanching is grown closely together in blocks to restrict light to the stems; the outer plants are often blanched with collars.

BEST VARIETIES

'Golden self-blanching' is an early variety with yellow foliage and cream stalks.

'Utah 52 to 70' is disease-tolerant with crisp, smooth stems and good flavour.

SOIL

Dig over the soil one month before planting, incorporating plenty of well-rotted manure or compost. A week or so before planting, rake in a handful of general-purpose fertilizer per square metre of soil.

For trench celery, the bed should be prepared during December or January, as weather permits. Dig a trench 45 cm wide and 30 cm deep. Put the soil on either side of the trench so that two ridges are formed.

SOWING

In February or March, sow the celery seed in modules filled with a multi-purpose compost but leave the seeds exposed. Keep the modules on a window sill. After the seeds have germinated, pot up into 7.5 cm pots and leave them to grow.

When the first true leaves have formed in May or June, harden the plants off.

PLANTING

Plant out self-blanching celery 23 cm apart in rows 23 cm apart.

Trench celery can be planted in the traditional way in trenches 30 cm between plants in two rows, 30 cm apart in a trench 45 cm wide. To grow trench celery with collars, plant on level ground, 30 cm between plants and 30 cm between rows.

Plants may need staking with a cane in exposed sites.

BLANCHING

When trench celery plants are 30 cm high, remove any suckers and loose, dead or decayed leaves. Tie the stems loosely below the leaves. Water the soil so it is just moist then draw the soil up until about 10 cm high around the stems. Repeat every three weeks until only the tops are visible. Don't earth up above the leaves and take care that no soil falls into the heart of the plants.

To blanch trench celery or the external plants of a block of self-blanching celery with collars, use 20 cm strips of black plastic lined with paper to prevent sweating. Tie the collar loosely to allow space for the stems to grow. Further collars can be added to extend the height of the blanch.

FEEDING AND WATERING

The ground should be well manured two months before planting. As the celery grows it will require several feeds with a nitrogen-rich fertilizer to boost the growth.

It is essential that the soil is kept as most as possible.

PESTS AND DISEASES

Regularly inspect your celery plants for slugs and remove any split stalks and sucker growth. A very dilute mixture of calcium nitrate will help to deter heart rot.

HARVESTING

Water plants well the day before harvesting. To lift celery, insert a spade on all four sides of the base of the plant, then, grasping the leafy top, pull gently. Remove the collar then use a hose to wash away the unnecessary dirt inside the stems.

STORING

Trim the base and remove any leaves or ribs that are damaged or bruised. Rinse, place in a plastic bag, and keep in the refrigerator, and it will last about two weeks.

CELERIAC

Apium graveolens var. rapaceum

Celeriac is a form of celery that grows with a fat, fleshy stem base that can be cooked or grated raw into salads. The leaves can also be used for seasoning or as a garnish.

BEST VARIETIES
'Prinz' is reliable and widely available.

'Praque Giant' is smooth skinned and hardy.

'Diamant' is a vigorous grower and stores well.

'Monarch' is a popular variety with good disease resistance.

SOIL
A well-drained soil that has been enriched with well-rotted manure the winter before planting. Ideally pH 6 to 6.5.

POSITION
Celeriac will tolerate light shade but will do better in a warm, open and sunny position.

SOWING
Celeriac requires a long growing season. Sow the seeds in a seed tray of compost in mid-March and keep at around 10 to 15°C. Prick out seedlings into 7 cm pots when large enough to handle. Keep the pots indoors for another month then harden off for two weeks before planting out in May.

PLANTING
Position the young plants 30 cm apart in rows 40 cm apart. Ensure the crowns are at soil level, not buried.

ROUTINE CARE
Mulch after planting and keep well watered. Towards the end of summer remove some of the outer leaves, as this will encourage the bulbs to develop.

Earth up in late autumn and in winter protect with a layer of straw around the crowns.

PESTS AND DISEASES
Celery fly, slugs and snails and leaf spot. Celery fly can be avoided if planting out is done from late May onwards.

HARVESTING
The bulbs are ready for harvesting when they are 10 cm in diameter. The flavour improves if the roots are mulched and left in the ground until March if the conditions are not severe.

Leaves and leafstalks can be used in place of celery in soup stock.

STORING
Celeriac can be stored in boxes packed in damp sand and kept cool.

KOHL RABI

Brassica oleracea (Gongylodes Group)

Kohl rabi is a Brassica grown for its swollen stem, which can be eaten like a turnip or shredded and used in salads or coleslaw. Kohl rabi literally means 'cabbage turnip' in German. It can be grown out of season in a polytunnel. It is easy to grow and makes both an interesting crop and ingredient.

BEST VARIETIES

'Kolibri' has a large stem with dark purple skin and is very tasty.

'Azure Star' is a very attractive crop with blue-purple stems.

SOIL

Can be grown on heavy soils but prefers a light, free-draining but rich soil. pH 5.5 to 7.

POSITION

Prefers an open site that is sheltered from strong winds.

SOWING TIMES

Sow in postion from mid-spring to mid-summer. Sow small amounts successionally to allow for harvesting from spring to the middle of autumn. Generally speaking, white and green varieties are best sown between March and June and purple varieties are hardier and better for sowing later in July and August.

SOWING

Sow thinly 1 cm deep in rows 35 cm apart. Kohl rabi is a fast-growing crop and is suitable for interplanting among slower growers.

THINNING

Thin as soon as the first true leaves appear and continue thinning until the plants are 18 cm apart.

ROUTINE CARE

Kohl rabi needs water through the growing season to prevent the stems becoming woody and unpalatable. Keep weeds in check. The crop does not require feeding.

PESTS AND DISEASES

Club root is the most common problem but kohl rabi can also be affected by cabbage root fly, cabbage whitefly, caterpillars and flea beetle, damping off, downy mildew, whiptail and wire stem.

HARVESTING

Pull the plants out of the soil when the bulbous stems are between the size of a golf and a tennis ball.

STORING

Trim the leaves and roots, then store in a cool, dry place.

THE ONION FAMILY

Onions are very easy to grow and have a long storage life, so they are a favourite among allotment growers. With a little planning they can be available for most of the year. They are also ideal plants for growing in small, confined spaces and particularly thrive in raised beds.

The onion (or allium) family is very diverse and contains more than 500 different species. As with many plants, it was the Romans that introduced the onion to Europe. Their distinctive smell comes from aromatic sulphide compounds. Garlic is the most pungent of this family, and has been used medicinally for centuries, particularly as an antiseptic. In fact it is believed that all members of the onion family play a role in lowering incidences of heart disease.

The ground needs to be well prepared to grow onions; particularly clay soils, which will need to be worked into a fine tilth with plenty of organic matter. Using a green manure ahead of planting would prepare the soil, and this should ideally be planted between March and September.

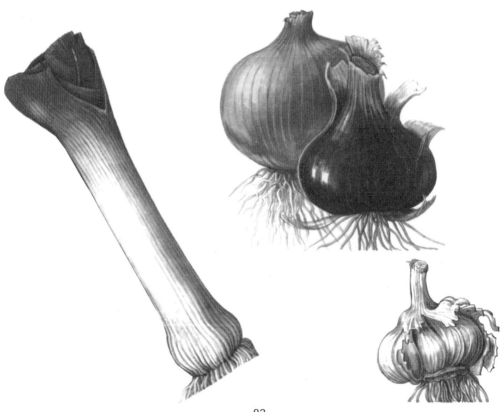

ONIONS

Allium cepa

QUICK REFERENCE

Soil
Onions prefer a free draining, light to medium soil that has been well manured. pH 6.0 to 7.5

Position
Full sun in an open position, sheltered from wind.

Sowing times
Seed can be sown indoors in modules around eight weeks before the last frost. Direct sow seed as soon as soil is reliably 10°C. Some seeds, such as the Japanese variety 'Senshyu Yellow', can be sown in summer for harvesting the following summer.

Planting times
Plant sets mid to late Autumn.

Spacing
2.5 cm for spring onions. 7 to 10 cm for plants and sets.

Pests and diseases
Onion fly, onion white rot and downy mildew.

Onions can be divided into three types: maincrop, Japanese and salad/spring onions. Maincrop onion seed or sets can be sown or planted in late February through to early April. Japanese varieties of onion seed or sets can be sown or planted outside in late August for harvesting in late June. Salad or spring onions can be sown from March to July for harvesting from June to October.

BEST VARIETIES

Maincrops
'Ailsa Craig' is a large, sweet onion that stores well.

'Bedfordshire Champion' yields large bulbs that store well.

'Red Baron' is a very popular red onion.

Salad/Spring onions
'White Lisbon' a popular variety with crunchy white bulbs.

'North Holland Blood Red' has a mild flavour and deep red colour.

Japanese onions
'Senshyu Yellow' are flat bulbs with yellow skins that are sown in late summer to overwinter.

SOIL

Onions grow best on fertile, non-acidic soil. Dig to 45 cm deep incorporating large amounts of compost or well-rotted manure and remove stones before planting. The soil needs to be loose, friable and free draining, especially for over-wintered crops. If your soil is heavy, consider creating raised beds for growing onions. Warm the soil with cloches before sowing seeds in winter or spring.

POSITION

Onions tolerate light shade but yield better crops when grown in full sun.

SOWING MAINCROPS INDOORS

Eight weeks before the last frost is expected, sow seeds four to a module, 5 mm deep. Keep the compost moist and position the modules in a warm, light place. When the seedlings are about 15 cm tall, trim them back to 10 cm to stimulate root growth.

SOWING MAINCROPS OUTSIDE

The advantage of direct sowing is that the plants are less likely to bolt or suffer from disease. The disadvantage is they may take longer to mature in colder climates. Dig out drills about 2 cm deep and 30 cm apart and sow the seed thinly.

Thin the plants to 10 cm apart when big enough to handle.

MAINCROPS FROM SETS

Sets are onion bulbs that have been kept artificially small by being grown very close together. Choose sets that have been heat treated to resist bolting. Plant sets in mid-spring. Plant 10 cm apart in rows 30 cm apart at a depth so that the tip only just shows above the soil.

JAPANESE ONIONS

Japanese onions look and taste like maincrop varieties but they do not store as well.

Apply a general fertilizer to the soil two weeks before sowing Japanese onion seed in late August. Sow 2 cm deep, thinly in rows 30 cm apart. Thin to 10 cm apart when large enough to handle.

Japanese onion sets can be planted from early September to mid-November. Plant 10 cm apart in rows 30 cm apart.

For Japanese onions grown from seed or sets, apply a general fertilizer in March and begin watering if the weather is dry. Ease off the watering as the bulbs begin to ripen in summer.

SPRING ONIONS

Spring onions are onions that produce bulbs that are no wider than the width of the leaves. Other onions can be harvested before the bulb has fully formed and used in the same way as spring onions. Spring onions can be sown in drills in a continuous row then lightly covered with soil. Sow at three weekly intervals from March to June to ensure a continuous supply. Spring onions make ideal crops for growing in containers or as catch crops for fitting in around other slower crops.

ROUTINE CARE

It is important to keep the weeds down to ensure a good yield. Hoe carefully because onions hate having their roots disturbed. Apply a mulch to help keep the weeds down and to conserve moisture. Make sure you don't cover any of the swelling bulbs as they need to be exposed to the sun. Cut off any flower stems that appear as the plant's energy needs to go into swelling the bulb and not making seed. Stop watering once the onions have swollen and begun to ripen.

PESTS AND DISEASES

The onion fly looks like a normal fly; it lays its eggs on the neck of the onion and the resulting larvae tunnel into the onion and destroy it. Hoeing around the onions regularly will expose the eggs. Thinning onions causes the scent of the onion to attract the fly. Thin onions in the evening when the fly is less likely to be active. Growing from sets removes the need for thinning and the onions are less likely to be attacked.

HARVESTING

Spring onions can be harvested when they have grown to approximately 13 to 25 mm across.

You can harvest your maincrop varieties from August to September, Japanese varieties from June to July and spring onions from March to October. The onion is

ready to harvest when the foliage turns yellow and tips over. Leave for another couple of weeks before lifting. Choose a dry day to harvest bulbs, easing them gently out of the soil. Lay them on the ground on some sacking, if possible raised off the ground by 25 to 30 cm on a wire netting cradle so that they can dry out. If the weather is wet, lay the onion plants in trays or on sacking indoors in a well-ventilated spot.

STORING

Japanese onions do not store well, so use them as freshly as possible.

After giving maincrops two to four weeks to dry out, inspect them and remove any suspect ones for immediate use. Store only undamaged, hard bulbs.

Onions can be stored on a rope. Tie on by plaiting the dried foliage to the string. An alternative is to store in net bags. Store in a cool, well-ventilated area.

SHALLOTS

Allium ascolonium

Shallots are related to onions, but are drier with a milder and sweeter flavour. A good crop for any allotment, they are easier to grow and more productive than onions.

BEST VARIETIES

'Pikant' produces high yields of reddish brown bulbs of excellent taste and is resistant to bolting and therefore good for early planting.

'Jermor' is renowned for its excellent flavour and cooking qualities.

'Topper' is a vigorous grower and produces bulbs that store for a long time. Excellent for cooking, salads or pickling.

'Eschalote Grise' is a favourite with many top French chefs.

SOIL

Shallots prefer a loose, free-draining soil with a pH of 6.0 to 7.5. Lime if at all acid.

POSITION

Grow in an open, sunny position.

SOWING

Sow in mid-winter to keep under cover and transplant in spring, spacing 5 cm apart in rows 30 cm apart.

Sow outdoors in position 2 cm deep in rows 30 cm apart in late spring and thin to 5 cm when seedlings are large enough.

GROWING FROM SETS

Sets can be planted from winter through to mid-spring, whenever the ground is workable. Space sets 15 cm apart in rows 30 cm apart; plant them with the tip just showing above ground. Smaller sets are usually more successful than large ones because they are more resistant to bolting.

ROUTINE CARE

Keep the crop free of weeds and water during prolonged dry spells.

PESTS AND DISEASES

Shallots have the same problems as onions.

HARVESTING

Harvest shallots on a dry day. Pull up the clusters of shallots, shake off any excess soil, and leave them in a warm, well ventilated spot, shaded from full sun to dry out and cure for one week.

STORING

Shallots can be stored in mesh bags. Keep below 10°C in a dry, well-ventilated location. They can be stored this way for six to eight months.

GARLIC

Allium sativum

Garlic is suited to growing on the allotment because it is relatively maintenance free.

BEST VARIETIES

It is a good idea to ask your fellow allotment holders to recommend a garlic variety that does well in the local growing conditions.

'Early Wight Garlic' is originally from the Isle of Wight so is good for British conditions. It is best used fresh but can be stored for up to three months.

SOIL

Garlic does best in a deep, fertile soil with a pH of 6 to 7. Before planting, dig the soil well to a spade's depth incorporating as much organic matter as possible to help with the drainage. Including some sharp sand will also help improve the soil. Add a couple of handfuls of bonemeal to every square metre. If you have heavy soil consider growing garlic in raised beds, as this will help prevent them becoming waterlogged.

POSITION

Grow garlic in full sun, as it needs to grow quickly to produce good-sized bulbs.

PLANTING

Plant in the autumn at least one month before the first heavy frost is expected. Plant the individual cloves pointy end up, 15 cm apart and up to 5cm deep.

Two to three weeks after planting mulch the bulbs and the surrounding soil with a thick layer of straw to protect from frost.

ROUTINE CARE

Remove the mulch in spring and carefully hoe around the bulbs. In late March and again in mid-May, feed the soil with a general-purpose fertilizer. Keep free of weeds and water only in very dry spells.

PESTS AND DISEASES

Onion eelworm, white rot.

HARVESTING

Harvest when most of the foliage has turned a yellowy-brown, around mid-August. Gently ease them out of the ground using a garden fork. Be careful not to bruise the bulbs or they will not last long in storage.

STORING

Garlic needs to be cured well before storing. Spread the garlic on a mesh tray and keep in warm, dry conditions for two weeks. Cover the garlic if rain threatens and shade if the sun is very hot. Remove the tops and keep in a cool, dry place.

LEEKS

Allium ampeloprasum porrum

Leeks are a great crop for cooler areas. They are undemanding, easy to grow and very versatile.

BEST VARIETIES

'Musselburgh' is one of the best all round varieties, is very winter hardy and has thick, long blanched stems.

'Varna' is a minature leek good for growing when short of space. It is delicious used raw in salads.

'North Pole' is a reliable, hardy variety suitable for late sowings.

SOIL

The best soil for growing leeks is a moist, light soil. Do not plant in freshly manured soil because this will make the leeks too tough and coarse. pH 6.5 to 7.5.

POSITION

Leeks tolerate partial shade but do better in full sun.

SOWING TIMES

Sow thinly in a seed bed in early spring, 1 cm deep.

TRANSPLANT

Transplant in early to mid-summer, when the seedlings will be about 20 cm high. Trim the tops by 5 cm to reduce transpiration. Using a dibber, make holes 15 cm deep and 23 cm apart, leaving 40 cm between rows. Drop the seedlings into the holes. Do not replace the soil, instead water the seedlings thoroughly. The amount of soil carried back into the holes by watering, should be sufficient to set the leeks in place.

ROUTINE CARE

Hoe the bed regularly during the summer, water regularly during dry spells and feed with a liquid fertilizer every two weeks. Remove any flower stalks that appear. During the autumn, draw the soil up around the developing stems to blanch them.

PESTS AND DISEASES

Onion flies, onion white rot and rust can affect leeks.

HARVESTING

Most varieties are hardy and can stay in the ground throughout winter until spring. Ease leeks out gently with a fork, otherwise they might break.

STORING

Leeks are best harvested as required and used fresh. Leeks can be kept in plastic bags in the refrigerator for up to one week.

FRUITING VEGETABLES

The fruiting vegetables that are most likely to be grown in gardens and allotments in the United Kingdom are tomatoes and peppers. However, more adventurous gardeners will also grow aubergines and tomatillos. All these vegetables require warmth to yield good crops and need to be sown and started off under cover. They usually do best if kept protected, but if you do decide to try them outside they should be given the sunniest, most sheltered spot available.

Crop rotation

Tomatoes, peppers, aubergines and potatoes should not follow each other in rotation.

TOMATOES

Lycopersicon esculentum

QUICK REFERENCE

Soil
Rich, fertile and well drained, low in nitrogen but high in phosporous. pH 5.5 to 7.

Position
Start indoors, and need a sheltered sunny spot in garden.

Planting time
Under cover February to March. Plant out April to June.

Spacing
Set plants 60 to 120 cm apart, depending on variety of tomato.

Pests and diseases
Blossom end rot or blight.

Quick tip
The larger and older a plant is when it goes in the ground, the more likely it will become stressed and not grow so well. Ideally they should be no more than six to eight weeks old and planted out at roughly the date of the last frost. Be careful: some nurseries start plants too early and they become leggy.

Tomatoes need plenty of sunlight, water and feed – supply these requirements and you will be rewarded with juicy, flavoursome tomatoes that taste so much better than any you can buy from the supermarket. Unless you have plenty of time on your hands, avoid cordon varieties (also sold as 'indeterminate'), which require side shoots to be pinched out so the plant grows with only one stem. Bush and tumbling types are easy and more suitable for growing on allotments.

BEST VARIETIES

'Gardeners Delight' is a very popular cherry variety because it is trusty and well flavoured. Another cherry type worth trying is 'Sungold'.

'Ailsa Craig', 'Alicante' and 'Outdoor Girl' are good for medium-sized fruit and suitable for growing outdoors.

'Marmande' is a reliable, outdoors, beefsteak tomato that needs a lot of support.

The Italian Plum 'Roma' makes an excellent cooking tomato and is easy to grow as long as it has a warm sheltered position.

'Tumbler' and 'Garden Pearl' are small plants intended for growing in containers and hanging baskets. They are very easy to grow and their size and nature of growth also make them ideal for growing along the edges of raised beds.

SOIL

Grow-bags are a favoured growing medium with many people but tomatoes can be easier to look after in well-prepared ground. Work a 5 cm layer of compost into the top layer of soil in the spring and warm the soil by covering with black plastic or shaping into a raised bed.

POSITION

Give tomatoes as much sun and shelter as possible.

SOWING TIMES

When the seeds are sown indoors, aim to sow the seeds so that they reach the stage where they can be transplanted outside three weeks after the last frost date. They will usually reach transplantation stage about seven weeks after sowing. Crops intended for cultivation in an unheated greenhouse or polytunnel can be sown in late February.

SOWING

Tomatoes need warmth to germinate, around 15 to 30°C is required. As soon as seedlings emerge they can be kept at 21° to 27°C on a light windowsill. When large enough to handle, prick out into 8 cm pots and keep at the same temperature.

PLANTING

When 12 to 15 cm tall with the first flower buds starting to open, plant out 45 to 60 cm apart in well-prepared ground, singly in 30 cm pots or two to three per grow bag. Plant deeply with the new compost level up to the first pair of leaves. Cordon and bush types will need the support of a cane.

FEEDING

Start feeding once a week when the first fruits have started to develop. Do not overfeed, as you will produce quantity at the expense of flavour.

WATERING

Regular watering is a key factor to success with tomatoes, as it is essential the soil never dries out. On the other hand, overwatering will result in split fruit. In hot conditions water a small amount, two or three times a day. Splitting of the fruit's skin and brown patches on the bottom of the fruit (blossom end rot) are symptoms of irregular watering.

CORDONS

A cordon tomato has a single main stem from which all the leaves and flower/fruit trusses grow. This main stem is tied to the support of a cane as it grows. Remove all side shoots as these will waste the plant's resources. These shoots grow from the leaf axils (between the stem and the leaf). Any side shoots can be rooted as a cutting to provide additional later-fruiting plants. It is also wise to pinch out the growing tip from the plant when it has four flower trusses (six trusses for greenhouse plants), as this will help the fruit ripen.

TRAINING TOMATOES

There is a variety of ways to train tomatoes, and any of them work well.

- Use a cage as a support.

- Train vines up a stake by tying the main stem loosely with twist-ties, or torn strips of old fabric, such as old nylon tights or stockings. Make sure the stake is put in the ground at the same time as the tomato plant so that you do not damage the root system.

- Tie the vines to a taut piece of wire suspended from a frame.

Whichever method you choose to train your tomatoes, make sure you check them at least once a week. All you need to do is gently encourage the growing end of the tomato plant round the stake or twine.

PESTS AND DISEASES

Blight can be a problem with tomatoes, so do not plant where you know there is a problem with blight. Don't plant tomatoes next to potatoes or in soil where potatoes have been grown in the previous season. Tomatoes share other problems with potatoes, such as cyst eelworm and viruses.

Tomatoes grown under cover may suffer from whitefly, aphids and red spider mite. Companion planting with marigolds can deter these pests.

HARVESTING

The reason that shop-bought tomatoes are sometimes lacking in flavour is that they are deliberately picked under-ripe, so that they are firmer and will transport and keep better.

You will need to learn how to judge when they are just at the peak of ripeness. There is a fine line between this state and that where the tomato is past its best.

STORING

Eat as freshly as possible. If you need to store them keep the tomatoes on a cool kitchen work top, rather than in the refrigerator.

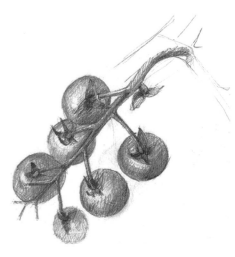

SWEET PEPPERS AND CHILLIES

Capsicum annum

Chillies are related to the sweet pepper and can be grown in exactly the same way.

BEST VARIETIES
Look for modern F1 hybrids that are bred to be suitable for cool climates.

Chillies
'Hungarian hot wax' is fairly reliable even in a less-than-perfect UK summer.

Sweet peppers
'Bell Boy F1' is very productive and yields a deep green, sweet fruit.

'Redskin F1' is a dwarf type that is good for growing in containers.

SOIL
Prefers a well-drained, fertile and moisture-retentive soil. Containers of multi-purpose compost with a little sharp sand mixed in are ideal.

POSITION
Give the plants a sunny, sheltered position.

SOWING
Sow seed under glass in late March/early April at 21°C. Germination may be quite slow. Prick out the seedlings when they are large enough to handle and pot on when

necessary. Harden off plants in late May or early June for about two weeks.

PLANTING
Plant out in position once they begin to flower. Space 38 to 45 cm apart or 30 cm apart for dwarf varieties. Cover with fleece or cloches to provide wind protection and extra warmth. Stake with three canes equidistant around the plant to support it when it is yielding fruit and tie in loosely.

ROUTINE CARE
Peppers naturally branch into two or more stems with a flower bud at the joint; if they don't bush out, pinch out tips at 30 cm.

Water little and often to keep the soil evenly moist and feed with a balanced liquid fertilizer once a week. If growing under glass, avoid temperatures above 30°C.

PESTS AND DISEASES
Caterpillars and grey mould.

HARVESTING
Pick fruits as soon as they are ready to encourage more fruits to develop. If you leave them on the plant, they will change colour and develop a sweeter flavour, or in the case of chillies become hotter, but this will decrease your yield by as much as 25 per cent.

AUBERGINES

Solanum melongena

Aubergines need a long, hot summer to mature but given the right conditions are very worthwhile. These plants can look ornamental when grown in pots on a patio, which confers the advantage of being able to move them under cover in cold weather.

BEST VARIETIES

'Black Beauty' is a popular, early maturing variety with purple-black fruits.

'Slim Jim' yields small, slender, quick-ripening. Very suitable for growing in pots.

SOIL

Aubergines require deep, fertile and well-drained soil. Warm up the soil with a black plastic sheet two to three weeks before planting out.

POSITION

Aubergines need warm, sunny and humid conditions. They are best grown in a glasshouse; if you grow outside give them your sunniest and most sheltered spot.

SOWING TIMES

Sow under cover mid-winter to early spring.

SOWING

Soak seed in warm water for 12 hours before sowing; this will help germination.

Sow seed shallowly in modules in good-quality seed compost. Germination is slow and needs a temperature of 21°C.

As soon as the seedlings are 5 cm high, pot them on to 7.5 cm plastic pots. Keep the temperature at 18–20°C. It is important to keep the plants in very good light.

PLANTING

Plant under cover of a cloche or polytunnel in late May or outside in June. Support with two or three canes and tie on loosely.

ROUTINE CARE

Keep well watered when the fruits are growing. Feed with tomato food every two weeks once the flower buds have developed. Mulch to conserve moisture, damp down polytunnels to keep conditions humid.

PESTS AND DISEASES

Aphids and red spider mites can be a problem when aubergines are grown under cover. Try companion planting with basil and/or marigolds as a deterrent.

HARVESTING

In a good year aubergines will be ready from August until October. Snip the fruits off with scissors when around 20 cm in length; picking them may damage the fragile plant.

TOMATILLOS

Physalis ixocarpa

Tomatillos are small, tomato-like fruits with a firm flesh. They are packaged inside paper-thin husks, almost resembling a Chinese lantern with a sticky outer layer. They are used mainly in making sauces and preserves and originated from Mexico.

BEST VARIETIES

'Verde Pueblo' has large, yellow-green fruits with a thin, non-bitter skin.

'Purple' has small to medium-sized, deep purple fruits with a sharper flavour than the green varieties.

'Grande Maje' has large, sweet, green fruits with good disease resistance.

SOIL

The soil needs to be loosened well before planting. Add a spadeful of compost to each planting hole and mix lightly.

POSITION

Tomatillos need a mild climate and sheltered area, so if you do not have a nice warm, sunny spot then the greenhouse or polytunnel would provide the best crops.

PLANTING

Start seeds in a heated greenhouse or propagator in early to mid-spring. Do not plant out until all danger of frost has passed. Cover the soil with black plastic two weeks before planting out to help warm the soil and promote growth.

PROTECTING

Make sure you cover your plants with some horticultural fleece for the first few weeks after planting to protect them from chilly air temperatures.

ROUTINE CARE

Don't overwater your tomatillos. Water them deeply once a week if the conditions are dry. Put a layer of mulch on the soil to retain moisture. You can also feed tomatillos with a balanced organic fertilizer or liquid feed when the plants start to bloom. You will need to stake the plants as they can grow up to 1.2 metres in height.

PESTS AND DISEASES

Tomatillos are generally problem free, but they can be susceptible to the same pests and diseases as tomatoes.

HARVESTING

Watch for the paper husks to change from green to tan or pale gold before harvesting. Green fruits will be more tart than those left on the plants until they turn yellow. The papery covering will split open when ripe.

CUCUMBERS & SQUASHES

Cucumbers are originally from Africa and Asia and have been used in India for more than 3,000 years. Courgettes are popular in Mediterranean food, while in northern Europe they tend to be grown bigger and used as marrows. Pumpkins and squashes are associated with North America, especially New England.

All of the above plants are classed as cucurbits and are grouped together here because they have similar traits and requirements.

Cucurbits have large flat seeds that need to be sown so that they are upright, not flat, which will prevent water from lying on the seed and rotting it. All cucurbits will benefit from being sown indoors. However, the faster-growing crops, such as courgettes, can be sown outdoors in position.

Seedlings that have been raised under cover will need hardening off for two weeks in a cold frame before planting out.

All of these crops require a warm and sheltered site. They all need phosphorus, too, so should be planted in the same rotation as tomatoes, peppers and aubergines.

CUCUMBERS

Cucumis sativus

QUICK REFERENCE

Soil
Well-manured and drained but able to retain water. They like a low nitrogen level.

Position
Any sheltered, sunny spot outside, can tolerate light shade.

Planting time
Outdoor types should be sown in mid-spring to early summer. Indoor types from mid-winter to late spring and transplant in early summer.

Sowing
Sow seed on its side at depth of 2.5 cm in well-manured soil.

Pests and diseases
Red spider mite, aphids and cucumber mosaic virus.

Quick tips
Keep weeds down around these plants and mulch ground to retain the moisture. Support the plants if necessary. Plants benefit from liquid organic feed during fruiting.

Cucumbers are the most tender of the squash family and are often overlooked by the allotment gardener, believing they can only be grown in a greenhouse. Some varieties, however, are hardy and are suitable for growing outdoors. Cucumbers can be divided into three types:

- The 'ridge' cucumbers that are grown outdoors
- The indoor cucumbers, which have a smoother and thinner skin
- The gherkin or pickling cucumbers, which are usually grown outdoors but produce smaller fruit.

Should you decide to have a go at growing cucumbers you need to bear in mind that they do take up quite a lot of room.

BEST VARIETIES

Outdoor types
'Burpless Tasty Green F1' is a good cropper, tasty and has good disease resistance.

'Long Green' is a reliable, good cropper with good flavour.

Indoor types
'Femdan' is a modern hybrid that does not require pollination to set fruit.

Pickling/gherkin types

'Venlo pickling' is trouble free and prolific. Suitable for growing outdoors.

SOIL

Work a layer of compost into the top several inches of soil. Warm the soil up before planting by covering with black plastic for at least two to three weeks.

POSITION

They need to be put in a sheltered position with plenty of sun.

SOWING

Start seeds in a heated greenhouse, frame or propagator in early to mid-spring. As they do not transplant easily, use peat pots to avoid root disturbance when planting out. Alternatively, sow six to eight seeds in a mound with 0.9 to 1.9 m between mounds.

THINNING

Thin seedlings or set the transplants 30 cm apart. If sown in mounds thin to three plants per mound.

FEEDING

Feed organic liquid feed when the plants are fruiting.

WATERING

Do not allow cucumbers to dry out, especially during the flowering and fruiting stages. They rely on moisture for good fruit development. A drip irrigation system is a good idea, as this keeps the soil moist without getting the foliage wet.

PESTS AND DISEASES

Red spider mites, whitefly, cucumber mosaic virus, grey mould, powdery mildew and soil-borne diseases.

POLLINATION

Outdoor cucumbers need to have female flowers pollinated by a male to set fruits. If you are growing them in a greenhouse, you need to prevent pollination or you will end up with bitter, inedible fruit. Grow all-female varieties, and quickly remove any male flowers if they appear.

HARVESTING

The best time to harvest cucumbers is in the morning, while the fruits are still cool. Don't allow the fruit to get too large or they can become bitter and the skin will be too tough. Do not leave overgrown fruits on the plant, as these will suppress the growth of new fruits.

STORING

Before storing, plunge cucumbers in cold water to chill them. Keep them in the refrigerator inside plastic bags for up to one week. If you want to make pickle, pick the fruits while they are still small and use them while they are still fresh for best results.

COURGETTES & MARROWS

Cucurbita pepo

QUICK REFERENCE

Soil
Well-manured and drained but able to retain water, with a low nitrogen level.

Position
Any sheltered, sunny spot outside, can tolerate light shade.

Planting time
Sow outside in early summer.

Sowing
Sow seeds in slightly raised planting mounds, a few inches apart.

Pests and diseases
Slugs can be a problem when plants are young. Cucumber mosaic virus and mildew.

Quick tips
Keep weeds down around these plants and mulch the ground to retain the moisture. Support the plants if necessary. Marrows are the same as courgettes, but they have been allowed to grow larger. If you wish you can let courgette varieties develop into marrows, the quality is just the same.

Courgettes, known as zucchini in the United States, are classified as a summer squash. You have to remember that if you forget to pick them, they will develop into large, tougher-skinned marrows. If picked small, courgettes have more flavour and a better texture. You can also eat the pretty yellowy-orange flowers these plants produce. They are excellent covered in batter and fried or stuffed and baked in the oven.

BEST VARIETIES
'Black Beauty' is a classic courgette with dark green fruits.

'Gold Rush' has a golden yellow skin and has a wonderful creamy flavour. It is a vigorous grower.

'Venus' is a very compact plant and therefore ideal for anyone who is short of space. It has glossy, dark green fruits.

'Zephyr' is a straight-necked courgette with slender, yellow fruits tipped with pale green. They have a wonderful flavour and texture.

There are several varieties that are smooth and spineless. Also look for those that are virus-resistant.

SOIL

Work a layer of compost into the top several inches of soil. If you are sowing seeds in mounds, then add several spadefuls of compost to each mound.

POSITION

Summer squashes do best in a warm, sheltered spot. Warm up the soil with black plastic two to three weeks before planting.

SOWING

Sow seeds in slightly raised mounds. Sow six to eight seeds a few inches apart. Sew the flat seeds on their edge to reduce the chance of them rotting in the soil.

THINNING

Thin each mound to the two or three strongest plants.

FEEDING

Feed organic liquid feed with a high-potash fertilizer when the plants are fruiting.

WATERING

Do not allow these vegetables to dry out, especially during flowering. They need plenty of moisture at the fruiting stage for the fruits to develop.

PESTS AND DISEASES

Slugs, cucumber mosaic virus, blossom end rot and mildew.

POLLINATION

You can improve the fruit by pollinating by hand if the weather is cool or cloudy. First identify the male and female flowers. You can identify the female ones as they have a small swelling at the bottom just below the flower. You can either use a cotton bud or a small paintbrush to transfer the pollen from a male to a female flower. If the weather is warm and sunny, there should be enough insects to do the job for you naturally.

HARVESTING

When the fruits start to appear it is worth checking them each day, as they grow rapidly and the quality declines if they are allowed to get too big. Use a sharp knife to cut the squash from the plant, leaving about 2.5 cm of stem still attached. Most summer squash have hairy stems with minute spines, so it is a good idea to wear gloves when harvesting to avoid irritation to the skin.

STORING

Squashes can be stored in plastic bags in the refrigerator for up to two weeks.

PUMPKINS & WINTER SQUASH

Cucurbita maxima, Curcubita moshata, Curcurbita pepo

There is a huge variety of shapes, sizes and colours of winter squashes, and if you have space they are well worth growing if only for their ornamental value. They are exceptionally easy to grow and once they start to develop there is no stopping their growth. Your children will love the big pumpkins to carve into Halloween lanterns.

BEST VARIETIES

'Table Ace' is early bearing and has dark skin.

'Cream of the Crop' has a creamy white rind; member of the acorn squash family.

'Waltham' and 'Butternut F1' are classic varieties of butternut squash.

'Blue Ballet' is a compact variety of Hubbard squash, bearing fruits that are half the size of some strains.

'Sunshine' is an orange variety of kabocha squash that resembles a squat pumpkin.

'Spaghetti Squash' is excellent for cooking. Boil and simply scrape out the flesh.

'Sunny Hallowe'en F1' has bright orange fruit and is great for pies and making lanterns.

TYPES OF WINTER SQUASH

Acorn squash
One of the smaller varieties, which can have green, gold or white skin.

Butternut squash
This is one of the most popular of the moschata-type squash. They are reliable to grow and keep exceptionally well.

Delicata squash
These are long winter pepo squash with green stripes on a white skin. A good variety for baking and stuffing.

Hubbard squash
Large, rather lumpy squashes with a blue-grey skin.

Spaghetti squash
Named for its stringy flesh, which separates into strands when cooked.

Kabocha squash
Large maxima-type squash with either dark green or bright orange skins.

Banana squash
Long, with grey-green or pinkish skin.

TYPES OF PUMPKIN

Mini pumpkin

'Jack Be Little' is one of the most popular of this tiny variety of pumpkin. They usually grow to about 10 cm across and are fun both to eat and decorate.

Jack-o'-lantern

These are the classic, large, round pumpkins that range in size from 0.9 kg to as large as 11 kg. 'Connecticut Field' is probably the best known of the large variety, but the smaller varieties such as 'Small Sugar' are great for cooking.

White pumpkin

These are much more unusual but have become popular with many people to use as decoration. You need to take extra care of this variety, as their white skin can discolour if they are under stress.

Giant or jumbo pumpkin

These can grow to an enormous size, with the British record weighing in at more than 410 kg. 'Atlantic Giant' is one of the best-known varieties used for competition. You would need a lot of room to grow this type of pumpkin, but if space allows it can be fun.

SOIL

Winter squash and pumpkins are best if they are grown on mounds, but you need to remember that both their roots and vines spread widely. Work a layer of compost into the entire growing area. These plants will also thrive if planted directly into a mature compost heap. Two weeks before you sow the seeds or put out transplants, you should water the planting area then cover it with black plastic to warm up the soil.

POSITION

They need a warm, sunny and protected position to grow well, and will not survive in cold, exposed spots.

SOWING

Mid-spring to late summer. They need the soil temperature to be at least 15.5°C. You will receive a better crop by planting seedlings rather than planting seeds directly into the ground. Plant 0.6 to 1.2 m apart in rows that are 1.5 to 1.8 m apart. If growing the larger varieties allow 1.8 metres between each plant.

THINNING AND PINCHING

Crowded vines are prone to disease problems so make sure you allow adequate space when planting. You can control their growth by pinching the growing tips after the first few fruits have set. If you find that your plants are producing too many fruits, they will compete for sugars and nutrients and the result will be smaller fruits. Remove

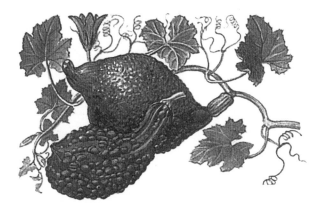

some of the more under-developed fruits from the vine to give the others a chance.

FEEDING

You should either mulch the plants with compost or apply a balanced organic ferilizer when the first flowers appear.

WATERING

Pumpkins and squashes need lots of water, or the fruits will not develop to full size. As a rough guide make sure you allow at least 10 litres of water to each mound every week. Make sure you soak the soil up to at least 30 cm deep. Once the plants start to cover the ground they will help to shade the soil, which means there will be less moisture loss. If you stop watering when the fruits are near to maturity, you will speed up the ripening process.

PESTS AND DISEASES

Apart from slugs attacking young plants, this family is fairly disease-free. They can suffer from cucumber mosaic virus or powdery mildew.

HARVESTING

The rind of a winter squash should be tough enough to withstand light pressure from a fingernail. Pumpkins should be harvested from early autumn, winter squashes from mid-summer, but both varieties should be harvested before the first frosts. Use a knife to cut the fruit off the vines, leaving about 5 cm of stem attached to the fruit. Make sure you handle them carefully, because if you allow the stem to break off it will leave a hole and the fruit will be open to decay.

STORING

To harden the rind, cure the squash at a temperature of 10° to 15.5°C, then move them to a cool area. Some types of winter squash can be kept for as long as four months in the right conditions.

POD & SEED VEGETABLES

Pod and seed vegetables, which include peas, beans and corn, are an essential part of any allotment garden. This family of vegetables will grow on most types of soil and produce an abundance of nutritious fruit. Some are grown for their pods, some for their seeds and some for both. They are decorative to look at with different coloured leaves and flowers and, because they tend to grow upwards do not take up too much space.

The taller varieties will need to be trained up some sort of frame, either a wigwam structure, trellis or fence. Dwarf varieties can be grown in containers if you want to put a few outside your shed.

Sweetcorn is in this family and is probably the most ornamental. It comes in many varieties some with multi-coloured cobs.

Peas and beans in general are exceptionally sturdy and can provide shelter for the more tender plants on your allotment. They like a sunny position and will need to be sheltered from strong winds.

One important reason for crop rotation is to make use of fertilizer left over from a previous crop. Peas are greedy feeders and they will benefit from the well-manured soil from last year's potato bed.

PEAS, MANGETOUT & SUGAR SNAPS

Pisum sativum

QUICK REFERENCE

Soil
Well dug and moist soil. If you know your soil is acid, then the addition of lime will help.

Position
A damp and cool spot, with some light shade.

Planting time
From early spring to mid-summer. If you live in a mild area also in autumn and early winter.

Spacing
Sow seeds 2.5 cm apart in two rows 15 cm apart. Allow 75 to 90 cm between double rows. Thin seedlings out to 5 to 10 cm apart.

Pests and diseases
Mice, birds and fusarium wilt.

Quick tips
Regardless of the variety of pea grown, they are best harvested while still young to retain their natural sweetness. Check vines daily if possible for any new pods.

Peas that are picked straight from the vine are so sweet that some people love to eat them as a snack. Sugar snap and mangetout can also be eaten raw and are a great addition to any salad. You will be surprised how different a fresh pea tastes to the ones that have been left standing around at the supermarket.

BEST VARIETIES
'Green Arrow' are excellent dark green peas on a semi-bush plant.

'Kelvedon Wonder' is a second early variety of sweet wrinkled peas that are resistant to disease.

Pea 'Ambassador' is a maincrop pea that has a long cropping period and is disease-resistant.

'Feltham First' is an early dwarf variety that is exceptionally hardy.

'Sugar Snap' is a variety of sugar snap pea with a sweet, fresh flavour.

'Oregon Sugar Pod' is a popular variety of mangetout with delicious sweet pods.

SOIL
Peas grow well in average garden soil.

Prepare the bed in the autumn, working a layer of organic matter into the ground. Shape it into a raised bed so that it drains away and warms up faster in the spring.

POSITION

Peas do not need a lot of sunshine, and prefer some light shade in a damp place.

SOWING

You can spread your sowing throughout the season by choosing different varieties. The early crops can be sown in autumn or late winter, but will need to have fairly mild conditions in a well-sheltered spot. The peas will do better if they are covered with cloches or polytunnels.

The main crop of peas should be sown from early to mid-spring.

WIDE AND DOUBLE ROWS

For consistent results it is a good idea to sew peas in either wide rows or double rows. For wide row planting dig a 15-cm deep drill down the bed and spread the seeds lightly in the base. Provide support for the peas down the centre of the row and thin out as needed.

To utilize double-row planting, dig two 2.5-cm deep drills about 15 cm apart. Sow the seeds 2.5 cm apart then cover. Provide support and thin as needed.

WATERING

Avoid watering peas excessively when the plants are still young. If the soil is cold and wet this could lead to poor root development and possible diseases. When you see flowers appear you can water once a week, but avoid wetting the foliage so water close to the base of the plant.

SUPPORTS

Providing supports for all pea varieties is essential. Either attach twine to some sturdy stakes or use chicken-wire. You can also use pea sticks which are thin twigs from trees and shrubs; this is a more tradional way of supporting peas.

PESTS AND DISEASES

Some varieties are prone to powdery mildew, root rot or they can be attacked by the pea moth. Mice, birds and fusarium wilt can all cause problems, too.

HARVESTING

Peas should be picked just prior to eating, as the sugars turn to starch the minute they are removed from the plant. Make sure you pick the peas while they are still young so that the pods do not get too tough. Harvest often to encourage new growth. Shelling peas are ready for harvesting when they are bright green and rounded.

STORING

You can store unwashed fresh peas in the refrigerator for two to three days, but they will continually lose their sweetness. Eat them straight away, or blanch some and pop them in the freezer.

ASPARAGUS PEA

Lotus tetragonolobus

Asparagus peas do not strictly belong to the same genus as peas and beans, but they are well worth considering on your allotment as they do not take up much room and can be an ornamental addition to any garden. They are hardy and flower from June to August, with the seeds ripening between September and October. Asparagus Pea is a very pretty plant that looks as good in the flower border as it does in the vegetable plot.

SOIL
This vegetable prefers a good, well-drained garden soil, and can withstand most soil types.

SOWING
Seeds can be sown directly where you want the plants to grow in mid-spring to early summer, meaning the seedlings are not at risk until the last frost is over. If you live in a cold area you might need to start the seeds in containers under cover, planting them out in early summer.

Sow 10 cm apart in well-raked soil in rows 30 cm apart. A little twiggy support is helpful but by no means essential.

WATERING
Water well if the weather is dry.

HARVESTING
After about two months you will see tiny pods appear that have four raised ridges with frilly edges. These pods have a taste somewhere beeen asparagus and peas, but only very young pods, less than 25 mm, should be used, as they become very fibrous as they get older and are not edible. Check the plants daily and remove any pods that are suitable for eating. If you pick the crop regularly, asparagus peas can provide you with pods for as long as three months.

COOKING
They can be used raw and added to salads, or cooked as a vegetable. They are best cooked as you would asparagus – lightly steamed with a little butter.

FRENCH & BROAD BEANS

Phaseolus vulgaris

French beans come in both climbing and dwarf varieties. They are very easy to grow and idea for those just starting to grow vegetables. They are prolific, the more you pick the more they will grow. Broad beans are another favourite with gardeners, as they are so easy to grow you can even get them to germinate on a piece of damp kitchen paper. Broad beans can be eaten in the same way as French beans, pod and all, as long as you pick them while they are still young and tender.

One of the great bonuses of broad beans is that they put nitrogen into the soil, so they are great for an area that is to be used for a nitrogen-loving crop the next year.

BEST VARIETIES OF FRENCH BEANS

'Purple Teepee' has dusky purple beans that are carried at the top of the plant.

'Tendergreen' a good crop of round, stringless beans, which have a good flavour and are ideal for freezing.

'Rocquencourt' has striking yellow pods and green foliage, making them a very decorative variety.

'Blue Lake' is a climbing variety with a wonderful flavour. It has white beans that are excellent dried as haricots.

'Royalty' is a bush variety that is best eaten young and it has a lovely fresh taste.

BEST VARIETIES OF BROAD BEAN

'Aquadulce Claudia' is a vigorous, old variety that produces white beans.

'The Sutton' is a bushy, high-yielding variety.

'Bonny Lad' is a popular variety because of its high yield and tender pods.

SOIL

These plants prefer their soil deeply dug and rich. It is a good idea to plant a green manure the preceding autumn. Dig it into the soil in spring and allow it to break down for several weeks before planting.

POSITION

They need a sheltered spot to flourish and will do better under a cloche initially.

SOWING

Always make sure you only sow really fresh beans, as their quality declines quickly. It is worth soaking them for half an hour to soften their skin, as this will encourage germination before you plant them. Don't be tempted to sow too many, as they are abundant croppers. Sow three small batches six weeks apart for a steady supply. Sow the beans about 2.5 to 5 cm apart in rows 45 to 75 cm apart. Thin out to 15 cm apart.

THINNING
Only keep the strongest plants. Weak plants are more prone to disease, which could quickly spread to the healthy plants.

WATERING
Keep moist when their flowers are setting and throughout the growing season.

FERTILIZING
You should not need to provide extra fertilizer for your beans if your soil has been prepared sufficiently before planting. Too much nitrogen can cause excessive leaf growth at the expense of pods.

SUPPORTS
You will need to provide support for the climbing varieties. This can be anything from a few canes to a more elaborate wigwam.

PESTS AND DISEASES
Green and black aphids love beans. Plant a few marigolds as companion plants, as they are particularly good at attracting aphid-eating ladybirds and hoverflies. As the aphids like to congregate on the tips of the plant, pinch out the plants in early summer. Slugs and snails can quickly decimate your crop, so take precautions.

HARVESTING
When you think it is time to harvest your beans it is worth sampling some first. The pods of French beans should be crisp enough to snap in half when bent. The tips, however, should be flexible and not snap when bent. The seeds inside the pods should be tiny. It is best to pick the pods while they are still young, as they will quicky deteriorate and the plant could stop producing if you do not pick regularly.

Broad beans should be harvested when the beans have swollen and are starting to show as bulges on the sides of the pod. The scar where the bean is still attached to the pod should be pale green; if it has started to darken it means the beans are too mature.

If you want dried beans, wait until most of the foliage has died off. The beans should rattle loosely inside the pods, which should have turned brown or brownish-black.

STORING
Most beans will last for up to one week if kept in a refrigerator, and all varieties of French and broad beans freeze well. Make sure dried beans do not have any moisture left in them before storing. You can test this by putting them in a closed glass jar for 24 hours to see if they produce any moisture. When fully dried, store in airtight jars in a cool, dry place.

RUNNER BEANS

Phaseolus coccineus

QUICK REFERENCE

Soil
Runner beans will thrive in a welldug, fertile soil with good moisture retention. pH 6.5–7.5.

Position
Give this crop a warm, sheltered spot that does not get frosted.

Planting time
Sow indoors in mid-spring, or outside as soon as the risk of frost has passed and the soil is at least 12°C.

Spacing
15 cm apart in double rows of 60 cm.

Pests and diseases
Slugs and aphids are the most common pests.

Quick tips
Dwarf cultivars can save on space and will not shade other plants like the full-size runner bean plant can. They do well planted in containers.

Plant a few sweet peas among the beans to encourage pollinating insects.

Runner beans are seen on every allotment, climbing up pyramids and providing beans month after month. The days of the old stringy beans are gone now that there are so many reliable varieties to choose from. They are exceptionally easy to grow, needn't take up a lot of space and make a showy display with their red or white flowers. Runner beans are one of those wonderful plants that thrive on being picked, rewarding you with more beans every day.

BEST VARIETIES

'Enorma' is a prize-winning variety that yields heavy crops of long, narrow beans.

'Crusader' a bean with a long season and an excellent flavour.

'Gulliver' is one of the dwarf varieties that is easy to grow with a good flavour.

'Red Knight' is a stringless variety that is a heavy cropper with bright red flowers.

'Desirée' is a popular variety that is stringless and freezes very well.

'Hestia' is dwarf runner bean, ideal for large containers. Its bicoloured flowers of red and white make an attractive bonus on top of the tasty beans.

SOIL

A deep soil that can hold moisture is the key to success with runner beans. Prepare a deep trench and fill with manure the preceding autumn.

POSITION

Runner beans need to be grown in a warm sheltered position. They can tolerate light shade, but will need a place that will encourage bees, so no strong winds. If, due to crop rotation or other factors, you need to plant beans where they may shade other crops, plant a dwarf variety.

SOWING

If planting outside, pre-warm heavy soils by covering with a cloche 4 weeks before sowing. Once you are confident that the last frost has gone, sow direct to a depth of 5 cm, 15 cm apart in a double row of 60 cm width. Alternatively, you can start them under cover in deep modules in early April and plant them out one month later, at the same spacings. If you want a continuous supply throughout the season, sow again outside in July to give you a fresh supply in autumn.

SUPPORTS

Most of the varieties will grow to a height of 2 metres, so supports are essential. Either put canes in rows or form the traditional wigwam. Because you need the ground to stay moist, apply a mulch around the base of the plants.

POLLINATION

Unlike French beans, runner beans will not pollinate themselves. They rely on bees to do the work for them, so plant a few sweet peas or other flowering plants among your beans to encourage these beneficial pollinators.

WATERING

Water copiously throughout the growing season and on no account allow them to dry out.

PESTS AND DISEASES

Make sure you buy from a good source as halo blight can be carried on the seeds. Slugs love beans, so you will need to put some slug traps around the base of the plants to keep them away. Blackfly can also be a pest, so planting Marigolds as companion plants is a good idea to encourage beneficial insects.

HARVESTING

Make sure you pick the beans while they are on the young side, as maturing beans will discourage the plant from producing any new flowers. Start picking from June onwards and keep picking until you have had your fill. As soon as the first frost is forecast, pick any remaining beans, dig up the plants and dismantle the supports.

STORING

Runner beans freeze well, so if you have a glut none need be wasted.

LETTUCE & SALAD LEAVES

There are many leaves that can be used in salads besides lettuces. Grow your own rocket, endive, chicory or mustard greens to provide qualities such as crunchiness, colour and peppery flavours.

Lettuces and salad leaves are full of antioxidants but to gain the benefits of these nutrients they need to be eaten as freshly as possible. The best way to achieve this is to grow your own. You can make successive sowings of different leaves and harvest year round. Not only will you know the leaves are fresh but also that they have not been washed in chemical solutions as some supermarket suppliers do.

The tastiest salads include a number of different leaves to supply a range of flavours, textures and colours. If purchased from a supermarket these mixed leaves would be more expensive but this need not be the case when you grow your own. If you grow a small amount of a range of salad leaves through the year, the diversity of the crop will mean that you are more likely to have leaves ready to harvest when you want them.

As well as crops that are grown solely to supply salad leaves, there are other crops that are dual or multi-purpose, for example: Use thinned out beetroot seedlings for salad leaves or take no more than a third of the leaves from growing roots. If your radishes go to seed, take advantage of this and grow this as you would do cress. When Florence fennel has been harvested, if the stump is left in the ground it will produce shoots that can be used in salads.

LETTUCE

Lactuca sativa

There are four basic types of lettuce.

The cos (also called romaine) has upright heads of sturdy leaves.

The loose-leaf does not form a head when mature, it is easy to grow and comes in a wide range or colours.

The crisphead has crinkled leaves and a tight, firm, round heart. It keeps well but is not the easiest type of lettuce to grow. Iceberg is a form of crisphead.

The butterhead has a loosely formed head of soft buttery leaves; it doesn't store well but is easy to grow.

BEST VARIETIES
Cos
'Little Gem' is a mini-cos that is fast growing and resistant to root aphid. Good for growing in containers.

'Lobjoit's Green Cos' is hardy and reliable.

Loose-leaf
'Green Salad Bowl' provides exceptionally good eating, but should be eaten fresh because it does not keep well.

'Red Salad Bowl' is a bronze version of 'Green Salad Bowl' and is reliable and good for repeat cropping.

'Lollo Rossa' gives a fantastic colour to salads.

'Green Oak Leaf' is good for growing through winter for cut-and-come-again.

Crisphead
'Webbs Wonderful' is an old variety that is still popular for good reason.

Butterhead
'Arctic King' is very hardy and suitable for growing through winter.

'Tom Thumb' grows well early under cover of a cloche. It is a small lettuce that can be grown on a window sill.

SOIL
Lettuces are not particularly fussy about the type of soil as long as it is able to retain water. The soil should be fertile but do not apply fertilizer or nutrient-rich compost, as this can cause rot.

POSITION
Many lettuces prefer cooler climates because they need lots of rain. So the key factor in growing lettuces successfully is to site them in a position that is out of the full midday sun. If they become too hot they tend to bolt.

SOWING TIMES

Some form of lettuce can be sown for the major part of the year. To ensure a continuous supply, sow every three weeks and make sure you read the instructions on the packets, as each variety will vary as to when it should be sown.

The sowing process is the same for all lettuce at all times of year, although when sowing in autumn for spring harvest, you will need to protect most types with cloches from October to January. 'Little Gem', for example, can be sown in a greenhouse or under a cloche in February and planted out in May for cropping in June. Carry on sowing at three-weekly intervals throughout the summer. September and October sowings can be made under cover again for harvesting in the spring of the following year.

'Arctic King' can be sown outdoors in September, and can be left out through the winter to be cropped in spring.

SOWING

Use a trowel to dig out a shallow drill 1.3 cm deep and 30 cm apart. Sow three or four seeds every 15 cm then cover the seeds with soil, firming it down using light pressure. If the soil is dry make sure you water your seeds well. The seedlings should start to appear in about seven to 14 days.

THINNING

Thin seedlings when they are large enough to handle so they are 25 cm apart.

ROUTINE CARE

Lettuce is easy to care for, the key requirements are water and weeding. They will benefit from a layer of organic material (or black plastic) which has been cut to allow the seedlings to grow through. This will help to keep the soil moist and stop the growth of weeds.

PESTS AND DISEASES

Aphids, cutworms, slugs and snails, wireworm. Damping off, downy mildew and grey mould.

HARVESTING

Lettuces should be harvested as soon as they are mature. They will bolt if they are left in the ground too long. When the heart of the lettuce starts to form a point and grows upwards, it is beginning to bolt and should be picked immediately. The easiest way of taking them out of the ground is to pull them by the roots using a trowel and then trim with a sharp knife.

If you are growing 'cut-and-come-again', then you should leave these in the ground and simply cut away the outer leaves from near the base. This will encourage new shoots to replace the harvested ones.

STORING

Don't wash lettuce before storing in the refrigerator; just brush of any loose dirt and keep in a airtight container. Wash before using. To stop the cut edges going brown, cut with a plastic knife.

ORACHE

Atriplex hortensis

Otherwise known as mountain spinach, orache is very similar in flavour to regular spinach. It is easy to grow and likes cool conditions. Although there are many similarities it is not botanically related to spinach. The colours of orache make it a worthwhile ornamental addition to any allotment. There are three different varieties – red, gold and green – all of which have completely different flavours. If grown together in a bed they make a wonderful display of colour; added to a salad bowl they make the dish come alive.

BEST VARIETIES

'Green Spires' produces green foliage with a slightly sweet flavour.

'Rubra' and 'Purple Savoyed' produce beautiful dark red leaves and have a strong spinach taste.

'Aureas' has yellow-gold leaves with a much subtler flavour that the other two colours.

POSITIONING

Orache prefers full sun to partial shade. In the rotation programme, do not follow or precede with spinach, beetroot or Swiss chard.

SOIL

Orache will grow in most fertile soils that have been treated with organic matter. The pH reading should be around 6.5 to 7.5.

SOWING

You can sow orache outdoors once the soil temperature reaches 10 to 18°C, or indoors three weeks before the last frost. Plant at a depth of 13 mm with 5 cm between each one, thinning out to 15 cm.

Sow seeds every two weeks starting in early spring and keep sowing until the weather starts to warm up. Although orache can tolerate warm weather you might find it loses a lot of its natural flavour.

COMPANION PLANTS

Good companions for orache are any of the cabbage family, celery, legumes, lettuce, onion, pea, radish and strawberries. They do not like to share beds with potatoes.

HARVESTING

You can start to harvest the leaves for fresh salads as soon as they are 2.5 to 4 cm in length. You can also steam orache leaves but you will need to leave them until they have grown to 7.5 to 10 cm in length before picking them for this purpose. You can either pick the leaves individually until the plant begins to flower, or you can cut the entire plant to soil level when it reaches about 15 cm tall.

CHICORY

Cichorium intybus

There are three types of chicory. There are sugarloaf varieties, which resemble lettuces; red chicory, which is also known as raddichio; and forcing chicory, which is grown deprived of light to produce edible white growths called chicons. Few UK gardener grow forced chicory.

BEST VARIETIES

'Palla Rossa' is a delicious and very hardy radicchio that looks great and is very useful as a winter salad crop.

'Sugar Loaf' is crisp hearted, tasty and is resistant to bolting.

SOIL

It is best to prepare your soil for spring sowing by digging it in the winter and adding plenty of well-rotted manure. Remove any weeds and large stones then rake to a level finish. One week before sowing sprinkle the area with a general-purpose fertilizer then rake it into the surface.

POSITION

Chicory will thrive in a sunny spot but will tolerate light shade.

SOWING TIMES

Seeds should be sown in July or August, for plants ready to be harvested from October to December.

SOWING

Stretch a piece of string between two canes to give you a straight line, then make a shallow trench about 1 cm deep. Sow the seeds thinly, cover, water and label. The seeds should take about two weeks to germinate.

THINNING

When they are about 2 cm tall, thin them out, leaving a space between each plant of about 15 cm.

ROUTINE CARE

Water well and do not allow the ground to dry out, as this could encourage your chicory to run to seed. Keep the crop clear of weeds.

PESTS AND DISEASES

Slugs and snails, caterpillars of certain types of moth.

HARVESTING

Use a sharp knife and cut off the heads of the sugarloaf variety. Varieties with red leaves should be harvested after a period of cold weather, as this is when they turn the lovely dark red colour.

CORN SALAD

Valerianella locusta

Corn salad is also known as lamb's lettuce or mache and is easy to grow as a winter crop. It can be grown as a summer crop but may run to seed if sown before late June.

BEST VARIETIES

'Large Leaved' is good for winter salads.

'Vit' has a pleasant, delicate flavour.

'Verte de Cambrai' is a strong and vigorous grower with small leaves.

SOIL

Corn salad is not fussy about soil as long as it is moderately fertile and moisture retentive but does not get waterlogged.

POSITION

Grow your corn salad in a sunny spot in well-drained soil.

SOWING TIMES

By sowing in March, April, August and September, you will get a fresh supply all year round.

SOWING

Sow the seeds thinly in drills, 1 cm deep with 15 cm between rows. The seed can also be sown in modules to be planted out in position later.

THINNING

Thin the seedlings or plant-module-grown plants 15 cm apart. Grow 2 to 3 cm apart for cut-and-come-again.

ROUTINE CARE

Keep the ground well watered during the first few weeks and hoe frequently to keep the weeds under control.

If your region is suffering from a particularly harsh winter, then your crop will benefit from being covered with cloches. This will ensure that you have a plentiful supply of tender, young leaves.

PEST AND DISEASES

Apart from slugs and snails this plant is virtually pest and disease free.

HARVESTING

Cut the head from the plant or harvest as cut-and-come-again. The plants are ready to harvest once they have produced their fourth pair of leaves; start using the leaves as soon as they are ready.

STORING

Store the leaves in a plastic box or unsealed bag in the salad drawer of a refrigerator. To keep these leaves fresher for longer, do not wash them; simply brush any loose dirt off before storage and only wash before use.

ENDIVE

Cichorium crispum

Curled endive is also known as frisée and has crinkly-edged leaves and a sharp bitter flavour. Batavian endive has a less bitter taste and flat leaves. The bitterness of endives can be reduced by blanching the plants before harvesting.

BEST VARIETIES

'Cour d'Oro' is reliable and does not need blanching.

SOIL

Endives do best in a light, well-drained soil that has been treated with plenty of well-rotted manure.

POSITION

Can be grown in full sun or partial shade.

SOWING TIMES

The curly variety is sown in June and July and the wavy-leaved Batavian type is not sown until August.

SOWING

Sow the seeds thinly in drills 12 mm deep and 38 cm apart.

THINNING

Thin seedlings grown for hearts to about 25 cm apart. Plants grown for leaves can be grown closer together.

ROUTINE CARE

Water regularly and thoroughly unless the ground is frozen. Keep weed free. This crop should not need feeding if grown in a soil that has had organic matter dug in, otherwise apply a liquid feed once a month.

BLANCHING

Most endives need to be blanched to make them less bitter and more suitable for eating. When the leaves are completely dry, tie them together and cover each endive with an upturned flower pot, covering the drainage hole to block out any light. After about 10 days in early autumn, or three weeks in winter, the centre of the plant should turn to a creamy-white colour and they are ready for eating. Use the endives as soon as possible, as the leaves with start to toughen almost immediately.

PEST AND DISEASES

Slugs, snails, aphids and caterpillars can attack leaves and roots.

HARVESTING

Endives can be grown as cut-and-come-again or hearting varieties are grown until the hearts are saucer sized.

STORING

Best consumed as freshly as possible.

ROCKET

Rucola coltivata, Diplotaxis tenufolia

Although rocket is known for being an ingredient in Mediterranean cuisine, rocket is very suitable for growing in the UK because it prefers cooler conditions.

If you like the taste of rocket you must grow it! It is very easy to grow and possible to grow all year round if you have a suitable spot indoors or a greenhouse.

In the supermarket rocket is quite expensive, and has probably been washed with a mild chemical solution.

BEST VARIETIES

Named varieties are available but there is not much to choose between them. The main choice to be made is to grow cultivated or wild rocket or both types. Wild rocket resists running to seed for longer and has a slightly milder taste.

SOIL

Rocket prefers a rich soil that is moisture retentive yet free draining.

POSITION

Give rocket a sunny and sheltered spot. The crop is good for growing in raised beds or large shallow containers.

SOWING TIMES

Sow outside from early spring until early autumn. Rocket can be grown year round, if you can provide it with the protection of a greenhouse, cloche or cold frame in the colder months.

SOWING

Sow thinly in rows 25 cm apart and cover with a sprinkling of fine soil.

THINNING

Thin to 10 cm if growing for whole plants or to 3 to 4 cm if growing as cut-and-come-again.

ROUTINE CARE

Keep weed free and water regularly. It will run to seed if it gets too hot or lacks water.

PEST AND DISEASES

Usually mercifully free from problems. Flea beetle can attack but will usually only inflict minor damage of a few small holes in the leaves.

HARVESTING

Harvest as cut-and-come-again or harvest the whole plant 4–5 weeks after sowing.

STORING

Rocket is best used freshly harvested but it can be kept for one to two weeks in a plastic box in the refrigerator. Do not wash before storing; only before use.

CABBAGES & GREENS

The brassica family is very large and contains not only the plants known as Western brassicas e.g. cabbages, broccoli and kale, but also Oriental greens such as mizuna and pak choi, and root crops such as radish and swede. This section deals with the cultivation of Western brassicas.

All of these brassicas can be grown in partial shade but should be grown in the sunniest spot available. The larger plants, such as Brussels sprouts, should be sheltered from strong winds. Firm soil enables the roots to anchor the plant. The ground should be retentive of moisture yet not become waterlogged.

Clubroot is the main enemy of brassicas; for this reason the soil should be limed if at all acid. The other problem for brassicas is cabbage root fly; the best prevention for this pest is to place collars around the stems of young plants.

Some brassicas, such as cauliflowers and cabbages have varieties that are specific for seasonal sowing. With a little planning you can be harvesting different crops all year round.

BROCCOLI & CALABRESE

Brassica oleracea botrytis cymosa

Broccoli means 'little sprouts' in Italian. Calabrese is a different variety of the same family, which produces green heads as opposed to broccoli which grows purple or white heads. The broccoli supermarkets sell is more correctly calabrese.

BEST VARIETIES

'Tenderstem' is quick to mature, each plant producing many small, spear-like sprouts.

SOIL

The perfect soil is a reasonably heavy soil that is rich in nutrients and has been recently dug. If you soil is lacking in nutrients it is worthwhile adding some fertilizer and bonemeal.

POSITION

Give these plants a warm sheltered spot.

SOWING TIMES

These plants can be sown from early spring to mid-summer; some varieties can be sown in autumn. There is a wide range of varieties, with differing sowing and harvest times, sp consult the information on the seed packet or in the seed catalogue.

SOWING

Calabrese and broccoli can be sown under cover early in the year but these calabrese do not transplant well in warm weather. From April onwards sow in situ in rows about 50 cm apart. Sow two seeds per station, 2 cm deep and about 30 cm apart, cover with soil and water well.

THINNING

Thin out the weaker plant at each station so you have 30 cm between each plant.

ROUTINE CARE

Both calabrese and broccoli are easy to care for. A layer of garden compost around the plants – not actually touching them – will feed the plants and also retain moisture in the soil.

PEST AND DISEASES

Club root, downy mildew, aphids, cabbage root fly and caterpillars.

HARVESTING

Start to harvest your crop before the flowers open. Make sure you pick both broccoli and calabrese regularly to ensure that the heads are at their tastiest and to encourage the growth of new spears.

STORING

They will keep for a week in a refrigerator, but are infinitely better if they are harvested and eaten on the same day.

CABBAGES

Brassica oleracea

QUICK REFERENCE

Soil
A fertile, well-drained yet moisture-retentive soil is required. A pH of 7.2–7.5 is ideal. Lime if necessary to deter clubroot.

Position
This crop tolerates light shade but give it full sun to obtain the best yield.

Sowing times
Depnding on the variety you use, seed can be sown under cover from January to September or sown direct outside from March to September.

Spacing
Spring cabbage: 25 cm between plants.
Early summer: 40 cm between plants.
Summer: 45 cm between plants.
Winter cabbage: 45 cm between plants in rows 60 cm apart.

Pests and diseases
Clubroot and cabbage root fly are the main problems affecting cabbages.

Cabbages are extremely hardy crops and are capable of withstanding temperatures that would destroy many other crops.

Because they are suitable to most temperate climates and soils, they are perhaps one of the easiest crops to grow.

BEST VARIETIES
Autumn/winter
'Tundra' is hardy and reliable.

Spring
'Hispi' is a fast grower with good flavour.

Summer
'Red Drumhead' is not only tasty but colourful and almost ornamental.

SOIL
Cabbages prefer a firm, moisture-retentive yet well-drained soil that has been prepared with manure several months before sowing.

Check the pH and apply lime if it is lower than 7.0. Cabbages will grow with a soil pH of 6.5 but with a pH of 7.0–7.5 you will reduce the risk of clubfoot.

POSITION
Plant cabbages in full sun if possible although they will tolerate light shade. Shelter from strong winds.

SOWING TIMES
It is possible to plan a succession of sowings

from mid-spring until late summer to ensure a long harvesting period.

Type	Sowing time
Spring	End of summer
Early summer	Very early spring (under glass)
Summer	Early spring
Autumn	Late spring
Winter	Spring

SOWING

Start off in modules at the appropriate sowing time and the plants should be ready for planting out around six weeks later.

Summer crops can be sown 2 cm deep, thinly in late winter in seed beds that are protected by cloches. Move to their permanent position in mid- to late spring.

PLANTING

Plant spring cabbages 25 cm apart in rows 25 cm apart; if growing as spring greens space 15 cm apart in rows 25 cm apart.

Plant early summer cabbages 40 cm apart in rows 40 cm apart.

Plant summer cabbages 45 cm apart in rows 45 cm apart.

Plant winter cabbage 45 cm apart in rows 60 cm apart

When planting, be sure to tread around the plant to firm the soil and then water well.

ROUTINE CARE

Keep well watered. Cabbages are quite greedy and need a lot of fertilizer during their growing period.

Cabbage are quite fragile, so be careful when hoeing not to damage the plant or the roots.

It is a good idea to mulch with straw to keep weeds down and help the soil to retain moisture.

PESTS AND DISEASES

Cabbage root fly, club root, slugs, cabbage caterpillars, wirestem and cabbage whitefly.

A tip to prevent club root is to plant a stick of rhubarb with your cabbages. You can also twist a narrow strip of tinfoil around the stem of your cabbages to help prevent cabbage fly.

Place a collar around plants when planting to deter cabbage root fly.

HARVESTING

Cabbages are ready for harvesting when the hearts are firm. Lift the entire plant with a fork and cut the roots off above the base of the lower leaves. Discard any outer leaves that are too coarse for eating.

STORING

Early types do not store well and should be used fresh.

Generally speaking red cabbages store better than green ones. Cut off the roots and any damaged leaves, wrap in newspaper and keep in a cool, frost-free store.

BRUSSELS SPROUTS

Brassica oleracea

BEST VARIETIES

'Cascade F1' is disease resistant and has a sweet taste.

SOIL

They will grow in almost any type of soil, but these plants are top heavy when fully grown so a firm soil is best to prevent the roots from being forced out of the ground. Brussels sprouts can be susceptible to club root if the conditions are too acidic. Ideally the soil should be pH 6 to 7.

POSITION

Brussels sprouts will tolerate some shade but must be planted in a spot sheltered from strong winds.

SOWING TIMES

Sow under cover in January for a crop in early autumn or sow in mid-April in a seed bed outside or in containers filled with compost for a winter crop.

SOWING

The seeds should be sown about 1 cm deep, 10 cm apart, and watered in well. Don't be tempted to overcrowd the seeds, as this will result in weak plants later on.

TRANSPLANTING

The seedlings should be transplanted to their final site when the danger of frost is past; about mid-May. The soil should have been dug over a couple of months earlier, in order to give it time to settle. Plant the seedlings 60 cm apart. Make sure the soil is packed firmly around the roots and water them well.

ROUTINE CARE

The Brussels sprouts seedlings are very easy to care for. Make sure they are watered well, but do not fertilize, as this will result in leafy sprouts. They do appreciate a mulch of well-rotted compost, and possible staking if they are exposed to strong winds.

If you find that some of the leaves have turned yellow towards the base of the plant, make sure these are removed, as they can be a source of infection.

PESTS AND DISEASES

Aphids, clubroot, cabbage root fly, caterpillars, pigeons and downy mildew may attack brussels sprouts.

HARVESTING

A hard frost will improve the eating quality of your Brussels sprouts. Remove them from the main stem by using a sharp knife, as pulling them off can damage the stem. Take the lower sprouts first and work upwards, as the lower ones mature more quickly.

CAULIFLOWERS

Brassica oleracea botrytis

Cauliflowers are possibly the most difficult to grow of the brassica family. They are hungry, thirsty plants and fussy about soil and position.

BEST VARIETIES

'Idol' is a compact, quick-growing plant suitable for growing in containers.

SOIL

This crop needs a neutral or slightly alkaline soil to do well. If necessary, add lime to get a pH of about 6.5 to 7. The soil should be moisture retentive but not become waterlogged.

At least two months before planting, dig the soil to a spade's depth and incorporate a good amount of manure or garden compost.

POSITION

Cauliflowers should have a site in full sun and be sheltered from the wind.

SOWING TIMES

For summer varieties sow under glass in January to provide a June-to-July crop. Alternatively, sow outdoors in early April and transplant in June for harvesting in August and September.

Winter varieties can be sown outdoors in May and transplanted in July.

SOWING AND THINNING

Sow very thinly in a seed bed, 1 cm deep in rows 40 cm apart. Thin to 7 cm apart when large enough to handle.

TRANSPLANTING

Transplant when the plants have five or six leaves and no more. Water the plants the day before. Lift the seedlings carefully, keeping as much soil around the roots as possible. For summer and autumn varieties, space 60 cm apart. Space winter varieties 70 cm apart.

ROUTINE CARE

Cauliflowers require copious watering. Mulch around the plants with rotted manure or garden compost three weeks after planting. When the curds have started to form, give the plants a top dressing of nitrate of soda.

PESTS AND DISEASES

Club root, cabbage root fly, cabbage gall weevil, wirestem, downy mildew.

HARVESTING

A cauliflower is ready for cutting when the upper surface of the curd is fully exposed and the inner leaves no longer cover it. If left too long the curds will break up as the flowers start to form.

HERBS

There is a large range of herbs available that are suitable for growing on the allotment. This is a diverse grouping of plants with many cultivation requirements, so there are bound to be some that will suit the growing conditions you can provide. Most of these plants will not be needed in big quantities, so you may find it easier to fit a few herb plants in around your vegetables rather than give them dedicated plots. The herbs that need the most thought about siting will be the perennials and shrubby herbs that require (semi-)permanent sites. Annual herbs will need planning for sowing and planting times rather than positioning.

SHRUBBY AND PERRENIAL HERBS

Rosemary is slow growing but will last for decades given favourable conditions so it is worth buying one or two reasonable-sized plants. It will thrive in a free-draining, light sandy soil that is not too high in nutrients and slightly alkaline. It is probably best grown in containers if your soil is heavy. It prefers sunny positions sheltered from strong winds.

Mint is very easy to grow and very worthwhile. Do not plant in the ground unless you restrict the roots because it is invasive; it is best kept in containers. It does best in a heavy, moisture-retentive soil. It will tolerate some shade but prefers full sun.

Mint is said to repel many insects and is especially beneficial positioned near cabbage and tomato plants.

Oregano is easy to grow and can be sown indoors from February to May. Give it a sunny position in light, free-draining soil. This herb is fairly hardy. This herb will attract bees to your plot.

Bay can be expensive to buy as a plant but this is the best option because it is very slow growing to start with. While still young protect bay from frost but after three to four years the plant becomes hardy enough for most UK winters. If you keep it in a pot for the first few years it will be easier to protect. Take care when choosing a planting position because bay will grow in to a small tree if allowed.

Chives are perennial herbs and very easy to grow. They do best in fertile, moisture-retentive soil. They are good for growing in pots or indoors on a windowsill. Planting chives alongside carrots may deter carrot fly.

Sage is another easy-to-grow herb. Grow from seed or cutting and give it a sunny spot and free-draining soil that is not high in nutrients. Prune it back fairly hard every spring to promote fresh growth. Sage attracts honeybees and repels carrot fly.

Thyme is easy to grow from seed. It requires a light, free-draining soil and a spot in full sun. It will entice bees and other pollinating insects ver to your plot.

Tarragon is an important ingredient in many classic Frenchrecipes. The most important thing is to ensure you get real French tarragon, not the Russian tarragon that isn't worth growing. Only buy tarragon plants, not seeds. It is not possible to grow French tarragon from seed, only Russian. Put the plants in a free-draining soil that is not too fertile. Do not water except in really dry periods. Tarragon is one of the few herbs that does not do well in containers, it grows much better in the ground.

ANNUAL HERBS

Basil is invaluable for many styles of cuisine. It is easy to grow from seed. Sow under cover in spring and plant out after all risk of frost has passed. Sow little and often through the year. Basil makes a good growing companion for tomatoes.

Parsley is one herb that may wish to grow in rows on it's own plot rather than fitting in around other plots. It is easy to grow, just sow in position, cover the seed lightly with finely sieved soil and keep the soil damp. Parsley seed can be slow to geminate; to speed it up, soak the seed for 24 hours before sowing. Parsley is a good companion plant for both asparagus and tomatoes.

Coriander can be used for both its leaves and seeds. Sow a small amount of seeds directly in the growing position every three weeks from april onwards. Mulch the plants to stop the soil drying out, which can cause the plants to bolt. Harvest leaves to use as freshly as possible. When the plant has gone to seed, wait for the seeds to turn yellow-brown then snip off the seedheads. Put a paper bag around the head and hang them up in a warm dry place. The seeds will drop in to the bag as they ripen; store them in an airtight container.

Dill is a great herb for using with fish, gherkins and potatoes and in sauces and pickles. It prefers full sun but is unfussy about soil; try growing a few seeds in any spare spot you have. It is best sown directly because it does not transplant well. It will attract many beneficial insects to the allotment and makes a good companion plant to the brassicas.

Chervil tastes a bit like a cross between parsley and fennel. It can be used in salads and sauces and is good with fish. This is a plant that thrives in shade and is therefore ideal for growing in otherwise unusable spots next to tall crops. Sow directly from spring until autumn.

OTHER CROPS

This section is about crops that require permanent positions, such as asparagus and rhubarb. These are perennials that will resprout each spring and give you endless supplies of delicious stems season after season. Jerusalem artichoke is slightly different because it is an underground crop that can be planted in a different position each year. However, many gardeners like to have a permanent spot for this vegetable as it is then easier to keep under control. Although sweetcorn is not a permanent crop, it is included in this section because it is a cereal and does not strictly come under any of the other categories. It will take up quite a bit of space so it is worth keeping a space free for this vegetable each year. It is delicious when cooked and eaten as soon as it is harvested. You will find the taste far sweeter than any you can buy in the supermarket.

At the end of this section are the strawberries – possibly the most popular fruit grown on allotments.

ASPARAGUS

Asparagus officinalis

Many people decide that growing asparagus just isn't worth the trouble or the wait, but those of you who have tasted it straight from the garden will quickly change your minds. Although it can be quite expensive to start and takes a couple of years to come into production, it is well worth the effort. It will continue to reward you year after year for up to 20 years. Because it is grown in a permanent bed it does not come under the normal crop rotation system, so you need to make sure that the bed is prepared correctly. Asparagus comes in both male and female varieties. The 'all-male' varieties will provide the highest yields because they put all their energy into producing spears rather than seeds.

BEST VARIETIES

'Jersey Giant', 'Jersey Supreme' and 'Jersey Knight' are all-male varieties that produce high yields. They are disease-resistant and do well in heavy soil.

'Connover's Colossal' is an old-time favourite with gardeners and is reliable even though it is not an all-male variety.

'Gijnlim' is a consistent performer which has the advantage of being an early cropper. You can pick the first succulent spears in mid- to late April, ceasing in July.

'Franklim' is another all-male variety with large, good-quality spears and a heavy crop.

SOIL

Before you plant test the pH value – it should be between 6.5 and 7.5. Loosen the soil then dig in a 2.5 to 5 cm deep layer of compost into the top several inches. Because the roots of asparagus can go as deep as 1.2 metres, you will need a good depth of soil. It must be well drained but asparagus can tolerate heavier clays that have been well cultivated. Dig in plenty of humus and some grit or sharp sand to help with the drainage.

POSITION

Asparagus will benefit from a sheltered, sunny spot so that they don't get damaged by the wind.

PLANTING CROWNS

You can start asparagus from seed, but it is easier to buy one-year-old crowns. Plant the crowns in April in a wide trench about 20 cm deep; shallow planting produces better results than those planted to a depth of, say, 30 cm. Allow 30 to 45 cm between each plant and if you have room for more than one trench, leave 90 cm space between each one. The crowns should be planted on mounds, allowing the roots to slope downwards and out. Therefore, the soil you have dug out of the trench should be left along the edge, as you will cover the crowns over a period of time as they start to grow.

After you have planted the crowns, fan out the roots from the mound into the trench. Cover the crowns with 5 cm of sited soil, then gradually fill in the trench as the plants grow until it is level.

ROUTINE CARE

You will need to keep the asparagus bed free of weeds and, as the plants are shallow, hand weeding is recommended. A mulch will help to suppress the weeds, and should be renewed every autumn. Water thoroughly in dry weather, but ideally drip irrigation is the best method of watering for the first couple of years. You should make sure the bed receives at least 2.5 cm of water every week until the plants are well established.

FEEDING

Fertilize in early spring and again when the harvest is over to stimulate the growth of ferns. Side-dress with an organic fertilizer or with compost.

AUTUMN AND WINTER CARE

Once you have finished harvesting, leave the spears to form fronds, which will help build up a healthy root system. Make sure you keep on top of the weeds. When the fronds start to turn yellow in late autumn, prune them down to about 2.5 cm and apply a thick layer of well-rotted compost to protect the bed over winter.

PESTS AND DISEASES

Asparagus beetle, rust and slugs.

HARVESTING

Wait until the crowns have been in the ground for two to three years before harvesting. If you are tempted to harvest before this, you will only weaken the plants and your subsequent crops will not reach their full potential. Harvest every other day, or even twice daily if the weather is very hot, cutting the spears with a sharp knife about 7.5 cm below the ground. Wait until the spears are about 10 to 15 cm tall before cutting. You can buy a specially shaped knife for cutting asparagus which will make your job easier.

Make sure you stop harvesting in mid-June to give the spears a chance to build up their reserves for following years. Confine your harvest to six to eight spears per plant in the second year, and double that in the third year. After that you can expect at least 20 to 25 spears to every crown.

STORING

Asparagus is best eaten on the day it is harvested, but if you do have to keep some then make sure you cool them down quickly. They will keep in the refrigerator for up to five days.

GLOBE ARTICHOKE

Cynara scolymus

The Latin name *cynara* means 'pointed stake' and is an apt description for this robust perennial of the thistle family, which can grow up to 2 metres in height. Modern varieties have been cultivated without spines, and their attractive flowers make them an ornamental addition to any allotment. They flower from July to August and have blue to purple blooms that add a splash of colour. Apart from their attractive flowers, globe artichokes are grown for their flower buds, which can be eaten when they begin to open.

BEST VARIETIES

'Green Globe Improved' is perfect for perennial plantings, as it is a heavy producer with 10 cm large round buds.

'Imperial Star' is mild and prolific.

'Violet de Provence' is similar to the Green Globe variety, but has an attractive purple flower with a more elongated shape. Good flavour.

SOIL

They need a rich, well-drained soil that is able to retain moisture. If the soil is too rich in nitrogen it can prevent the globe artichoke from flowering. Loosen the soil to a depth of 30 cm and make sure you remove all perennial weeds. Spread a 15-cm layer of compost and work it into the soil.

POSITION

Globe artichokes need a position in full sunlight. They will be damaged by heavy frost or snow, so will need protecting in areas where the temperature drops suddenly.

PLANTING

Artichokes can be grown from offshoots, suckers or seed. For best results it is advisable to start with offshoots or suckers from a reputable garden centre. Planting in the spring is best, but you can usually judge when the offshoots become available at your local nursery. Set the offshoots with their crowns just above soil level.

ROUTINE CARE

Globe artichokes bear the best crop in their second year, and it is advisable to start new plants every three to four years. If you live in an area that has cold winters, you will need to cut the plant back to about 25 cm then cover it with horticultural fleece. Place mulch around the base to a thickness of about 50 cm to help to retain the soil's moisture and temperature.

WATERING

Artichokes will quickly wilt when deprived

of water. The foliage will quickly recover after watering, so make sure you water well during dry spells and during the active growing period.

FEEDING

Both annual and perennial varieties will need feeding monthly during their growing period. Give them a balanced liquid or organic fertilizer.

AUTUMN CARE

After harvesting in late autumn the leaves will start to die back. You can leave these in place to provide a little protection if you live in an area where the winters are generally mild.

PESTS AND DISEASES

Globe artichokes are generally trouble-free but they can be attacked by slugs and snails, which can easily damage young shoots as they start to appear in spring. If you see brown spots on any buds, it could be petal blight caused by botrytis. Remove and destroy any affected buds immediately. Occasionally artichokes can be affected by aphids, so wash them with a strong stream of water to get rid of them.

HARVESTING

It is a good idea to allow artichokes to build up their strength in the first year by removing the flower buds as soon as you see them. In the second and third year, cut the flower buds when the scales are still tight and waxy and the tips of the scales at the base of the bud are starting to lift. Use a sharp knife and cut through the stem about 2.5 to 5 cm below the bud. If you allow your artichoke to flower, you will inhibit the production of new buds. However, the plants are so attractive you might like to grow one and allow it to go into flower without harvesting.

STORING

Globe artichokes are best eaten as soon as they are picked. They will store in the refrigerator for up to two weeks.

JERUSALEM ARTICHOKE

Helianthus tuberosus

Although called an artichoke, the Jerusalem artichoke bears no relation to the Globe artichoke. It is a member of the sunflower family, *girasole*, and this plant produces tubers that have a nutty flavour and crisp texture similar to water chestnuts.

BEST VARIETIES

The best variety by far is 'Fuseau', which is not so knobbly and easier to cook.

SOIL

They grow best in rich, sandy loam but can live in clay or sandy soils if treated with sufficient organic matter.

POSITION

Be careful when positioning Jerusalem artichokes, as they can grow to more than 2 metres in height. The stems are fragile so you will need to provide support in windy positions. They are sun lovers and and benefit from being in an open sunny position.

PLANTING

Plant individual tubers to a depth of about 7.5 to 10 cm, 40 to 60 cm apart. These plants are vigorous, so make sure you plant this crop in the same place each year. It will be easy to miss any tubers from the previous year as it will grow rapidly, even if you only left a tiny portion in the ground.

ROUTINE CARE

Water the plants until they are well established and mulch the soil to conserve its moisture. Once established they will not require watering unless it has been a particularly dry spell. They like rich feeding, but as long as the soil has been worked with sufficient compost they should not need any extra nutrients.

PESTS AND DISEASES

Problems with Jerusalem artichokes are rare.

HARVESTING

It is best to leave the tubers in the ground until they are needed because of their thin skins, and they benefit from a few autumn frosts. To extend harvest into winter, you can leave a few main roots in place and mulch them well.

STORING

They will keep for up to two weeks in the salad compartment of the fridge. You can also store them in a paper bag in a cool, dark cupboard or cellar. One small point to bear in mind is that Jerusalem artichokes are renowned for causing flatulence, so try eating a small amount until your system gets used to them!

RHUBARB

Rheum x hybridum

Rhubarb is one of the hardiest plants that you can grow on an allotment. They can stay in the same position for up to ten years, and because the soil immediately surrounding this plant cannot be dug, you will need to bear this in mind when choosing the site.

BEST VARIETIES

'Glaskin's Perpetual' is a reliable strain to grow from seed, and provides good crops with bright red stems.

'Victoria' is a good non-stringy variety with green stalks that have a rosy sheen at the base.

'Champagne' is an early variety with a sweet-tasting, pink-tinged stem.

'Stockbridge Arrow' is largely trouble-free with a long cropping season. It produces tender, red-pink stems.

SOIL

Rhubarb can tolerate most soil conditions, but it does prefer neutral soil that has been dug to a depth of 20 cm or more. Incorporate as much organic matter as possible during digging, because this has to last the rhubarb plant for the remainder of its life. The site should be prepared at least four weeks in advance of planting to give it time to settle.

POSITION

If possible, grow rhubarb in full sun.

PLANTING

You can grow rhubarb from seed, but it can take a long time to get established. It is probably better to start off with a plant from your local garden centre, as they are available to buy all year round. The best time to plant out is in the winter, as rhubarb needs cold weather before it starts to grow.

Loosen the soil in the plant area to a depth of about 25 cm. If you are worried about wet conditions, create planting mounds raised about 15 cm above the surrounding soil. Put the plants in the mounds so that the buds are just below the surface of the soil. Gently firm the soil round the plant, making sure that no air pockets remain.

If you are growing from seed, start them indoors in late winter for planting out in spring.

ROUTINE CARE

Rhubarb needs very little routine care. Water well in dry conditions but do not allow the ground to become soggy. After the stems emerge, lay about 10 cm of clean straw, compost or mulch around the plants, making sure you leave the top free where the buds are emerging. Remove any weeds as they appear. Cut off any flowerheads that appear in early spring as the new rhubarb stalks start to emerge.

Rhubarb that is five years old or more, can be dug up and split into three or four separate plants.

AUTUMN AND WINTER CARE

Clear away all stalks and leaves in autumn to prevent disease organisms from overwintering. After the soil freezes, cover the crowns with a straw mulch. Remove half the mulch in spring before new growth emerges.

PESTS AND DISEASES

Because rhubarb is such a healthy plant it suffers from very few pests and diseases. The only problem you might come across is crown rot, which is where the top of the plant rots badly and it can be knocked off with ease. There is no cure for this so you will need to dig up the infected plant and burn it.

FORCING RHUBARB

Forced rhubarb is delicious as the stems are more tender, sweeter and do not need to be peeled. All you need to do is get a bucket, clay pot or large box – anything that is large enough to totally exclude the light. Place it over the top of the rhubarb as soon as it shows any sign of growth. The lack of light and extra warmth provided by the container, will rapidly force the rhubarb to grow. It should be ready for eating in about four weeks.

HARVESTING

Although it is very tempting, do not pull any stems during the first season, as this will seriously weaken the plant. During the second season only pull a few stems; do this by pulling gently as close as possible to the base of the plant and at the same time twisting. The leaves are poisonous so do not eat them, but they are safe to go on the compost heap. When most of the stalks are starting to get thin, it is time to stop harvesting for that year.

STORING

Rinse the stems with water or wipe clean with moist paper towels. Stalks stored in perforated plastic bags in the refrigerator will last for up to two weeks. Rhubarb is also suitable for freezing.

SWEETCORN

Zea Mays

Sweetcorn is not difficult to grow and will reward you with the most amazing sweet kernels if eaten the same day that they are picked.

BEST VARIETIES

'Jubilee' gives a high yield with deep, narrow kernels.

'Champ' is F1 hybrid that produces large, golden cobs. It is also tolerant of cold weather.

'Honey Bantam' is an early, sweet variety with multi-coloured kernels.

'Swift' is a very sweet, early, extra tender variety that is suitable for cooler conditions.

'Minipop' is a baby corn variety that should be harvested as soon as the tassels start to show. Great tasting either raw or in stir-fries.

SOIL

Prepare the soil in March to allow it to settle before planting. Make raised beds and add compost and nitrogen supplements. Ideally plant a green manure such as alfalfa or clover the preceding autumn. Leave the crop in place during the winter and dig it into the soil two weeks before planting.

POSITION

It needs to grow in a sunny position, but will grow in any soil that has been enriched with well-rotted compost. Sweetcorn plants are shallow rooted, so they will need protection from strong wind. Make sure the ground does not lose excessive water.

PLANTING

For sweetcorn to perform well it needs a long, warm season, so do not plant out until the last frost has passed. It also pollinates better if it is planted in a block as opposed to a row. Sweetcorn can be grown directly into open ground in late May, but you will probably have more success if you start sowing in pots under glass in April. Sow the seeds two at a time and 12 mm deep in pots filled with a moist seed compost. Cover the pots with newspaper and glass and leave until the seeds start to germinate. Sweetcorn does not like to have its roots disturbed, so it is best to start the plants in peat pots that you can plant directly into their final position. Wait until the soil temperature is above 15°C before planting out.

ROUTINE CARE

Sweetcorn will need to be watered well during grain development, especially in hot, dry weather. It also appreciates being fed once a fortnight with a fertilizer that is

EXTRA-SWEET VARIETIES

Sweetcorn comes in various varieties of sweetness – regular called 'sugary', sugar-enhanced or supersweet. Sugar-enhanced varieties have the same amount of sweetness as the regular varieties, but retain their sweetness longer after harvesting. Supersweet are much sweeter than the regular varieties and retain their crispness and sweetness better than the other types when they are frozen.

Supersweet seedlings are less vigorous and much more sensitive to the cold. You would also need to make sure that supersweet varieties are not grown in close proximity to other varieties, as cross-pollination can result in under-developed ears. You would need to make sure they are at least 120 metres away from maize or other sweetcorn.

There is another variety known as 'tendersweet', which has a very thin skin covering the kernels. This variety retains its sweetness after picking.

There are also varieties with multi-coloured kernels, which make a pleasant variation from the normal creamy yellow kernels.

You can also grow popcorn as you would regular sweetcorn. They require the same general attention, but can be left on the plant until it turns cold.

designed for tomatoes. When the stalks reach around 30 cm in height, use a hoe to earth up extra soil around the base.

PESTS AND DISEASES

Sweetcorn is usually free of pests, but it is still a good idea to watch out for greenfly, aphids and slug damage.

HARVESTING

You can test sweetcorn for ripeness by pressing your fingernail into one of the kernels. If it is ready for harvesting, it will release a creamy coloured liquid. If the liquid is still watery in appearance, then you need to give the sweetcorn longer to ripen. If the liquid has taken an almost dough-like consistency, then you have allowed them to get too ripe. Start testing as soon as the long silky threads turn brown and start to shrivel.

Try to pick and eat on the same day so that you can appreciate the full flavour and sweetness of this delicious vegetable.

Ornamental varieties are best left on the plant until there have been a couple of frosts. They can be picked after the outer leaves surrounding the cobs have started to turn brown and dry. Make sure they are hard and glossy before picking. Remove the husks and leave them to dry in a well-ventilated place for a few weeks before using as popcorn.

STORING

Sweetcorn freezes exceptionally well, but it is still best eaten on the day of picking.

STRAWBERRIES

Fragaria spp.

Strawberries will always be a favourite, with their sweet and succulent flesh. They are easy to grow and can be enjoyed from early spring to early winter by planting a variety of cultivars. Cultivars are broken down into the growing seasons – 'summer' produce fruit in the short days of late summer and early autumn'; 'perpetual' in the longer summer days; while 'alpine' make a great ornamental border with smaller fruit.

THE STRAWBERRY BED

Strawberries love a free-draining, fertile loam, so the soil needs to be well prepared before planting. Add a fresh layer of rich compost to the top soil, then fork it in to loosen the soil. Rake level. Avoid planting strawberries in the shade, as they need the sun to give sweetness to the fruit. Make sure that your bed is free from perennial weeds.

You can grow strawberries through a sheet mulch, which helps keep the weeds at bay, warms the soil and helps to retain moisture. Prepare the soil underneath to a fine tilth and mound it so that the water will run off the plastic. Keep the plastic sheet taut to get the maximum warming effect. Because the plants will quickly fill the holes in the sheet, you will need to install some kind of water system. It can be as simple as sinking plastic bottles with

their bottoms cut off through holes in the sheet in order to apply water.

You can purchase dormant strawberry crowns at your local garden centre. Space the crowns 15 to 20 cm apart in rows that are 20 to 30 cm apart, being careful not to plant the crowns too deeply.

ROUTINE MAINTENANCE

During the first growing season, pinch off flowers and runners to help establish the bed. You might need to cover the plants to protect them against weather and birds and other pests. Lift the cover during the day to allow pollinating insects to do their work.

Crops that are being grown on a flat bed will need protection from a mulch of straw. This should be removed in the autumn, as it can be a perfect home for slugs and botrytis.

As the crowns get older you will need to thin them out. Do this by pulling off smaller crowns at the base of the plant to leave three or four crowns per plant. This will help the plant to concentrate on producing more fruit next season. Also pinch out any dead leaves, old runners or rotting fruit to eliminate pests and diseases, such as strawberry virus and botrytis.

Expect to pick around 450 g of fruit from healthy plants. Picking when daytime temperatures are at their highest will give you sweetest fruit.

Pests and Diseases

TROUBLESHOOTING

At some time or another you will come across problems with pests and diseases when growing fruit and vegetables. It might only be a minor problem that can be dealt with promptly, while others will need more serious action. This section lists most of the common pests and diseases you will encounter and offers advice on how to deal with them.

APHIDS

These will probably be the most common pest you will come across on the allotment. They weaken plants by sucking out the plant's natural sap, causing new growth to become deformed. They breed rapidly, so you will need to take action immediately.

You will find they live in colonies under the leaves and on new growth, and if you see sooty mould then it is a sign your plants are infected with aphids.

Natural control of aphids

There are several natural methods of getting rid of aphids without using harsh chemicals.

- On plants such as broad beans where they are easy to see, you can physically wash them off, and pinch off the tips of the plants before the colonies start to form.
- The easiest method of dealing with aphids is to encourage predatory insects, such as ladybirds, lacewings, hoverflies and the ground beetle. You can buy special boxes that attract these insects. By providing them somewhere to spend the winter you are encouraging them to stay on your site.
- You can also plant a range of companion plants (see page 56) that will encourage these beneficial insects and these include: camomile, chervil, fennel, catnip, dill, mustard, mint, hyssop, tansy and marigolds.
- To encourage ground beetles, you will need to provide them with somewhere to live. The easiest method is to put a pile of logs up against a wall or fence. This little insect is also attracted to clover, so you

might like to leave a little bit of your allotment natural and grow some wild flowers.

ASPARAGUS BEETLES

These are small beetles with distinctive yellow and black markings. The adult beetle and larvae feed on asparagus leaves, eventually destroying the plant.

Natural control of asparagus beetles

- After harvest make sure you pick up all debris and turn the soil over around the plants to disturb overwintering beetles.
- Start checking plants in early May or just after plants emerge. Harvest the spears as early as possible.
- Beneficial insects, such as ladybirds and lacewings, will eat the eggs and small larvae.
- Hand pick the adults and immature larvae from the plants and drop them in a pan of soapy water.
- Remove dark brown eggs from asparagus spears.

BLIGHT

Blight affects potato crops and outdoor tomatoes, especially if the season is particularly wet. It can be identified by the brown patches that appear on the leaves and eventually leads to rot.

Natural control of blight

- Prevent blight by growing disease-resistant varieties.
- If you do find the first signs of blight, dig the plants up and burn immediately to prevent it from spreading.

BLOSSOM END ROT

Blossom end rot is a disorder that affects tomatoes, peppers and aubergines. It starts with a small water-soaked area at the blossom end of the fruit. As the lesion develops, it grows bigger and becomes sunken, turning black and leathery. It is caused by a parasitic organism and is associated with a low concentration of calcium in the fruit. It is also associated with underwatering when the fruit are grown in pots or growbags.

Natural control of blossom end rot

- Maintain the soil pH around 6.5 and add lime.
- Regular watering and feeding of pots and growbags should prevent blossom end rot.
- Use a nitrate nitrogen as a fertilizer.
- Avoid drought and fluctuations in soil moisture by using mulches.

BOTRYTIS (OR GREY MOULD)

Botrytis can attack a wide range of vegetables including lettuces, tomatoes and cucumbers, especially ones grown in greenhouses. Plants that have any cuts in their stems or leaves seem to be particularly vulnerable, so handle young seedlings with care. It is also known as grey mould after the characteristic fluffy grey growth that appears on the surface of affected plants. It is very difficult to get rid of once it takes hold, so prevention is the best cure. Try to avoid the conditions which suit it best, that is, cool, damp and poorly ventilated conditions.

Natural control of botrytis

- Ensure your greenhouse is well ventilated.
- Do not overcrowd your plants.
- Water carefully and not too much.
- Make sure your tools and hands are cleaned after touching affected plants.
- Clear up any debris as this could host the spores.
- Dig up and burn any affected plants.
- Remove any soil that can possibly re-infect new plants.

CABBAGE ROOT FLIES

These little white grubs of the root fly attack all types of brassicas and radishes, too. They bore into the roots of the plant, stunting its growth and making it wilt as it becomes weak. The flies are most common in spring, but they multiply so rapidly that they can be a problem throughout the entire growing season. Prevention is the best cure as there are no known organic treatments.

Natural control of cabbage root flies

- Put collars around the stems of the plants to prevent the fly from laying its eggs on the soil. Thick cardboard works well, or anything that will not rot too quickly.
- Cover your plants with horticultural fleece.

- Burn all infected plants and do not plant brassicas on the same site for three years.

CANKER BACTERIA

This disease can attack apples, cherries and plum trees. It enters the tree through cuts or wounds, and causes the leaves and flowers to shrivel up and die. The first signs of canker bacteria is a gold-coloured gum oozing from a wound on a branch or trunk of the tree. Frost damage in the spring may promote further infection.

Natural control of canker bacteria

- Prune when the trees are flowering, as the wounds will heal faster.
- Cut off the limb well below the affected area and paint the wound with an appropriate paint.
- Disinfect all pruning equipment after each cut.

CARROT FLIES

Carrot flies lay their eggs which hatch and eat their way into the carrots. You will see evidence of carrot flies from their brown tunnels. The carrot fly is attracted by the smell of bruised carrot leaves, so take care when thinning out or cropping carrots.

Natural control of carrot flies

- Sow in early summer and cover with horticultural fleece.
- Erect a barrier of polythene about 1 metre high around the carrots. This is effective

because the carrot fly only flies low to the ground.

- Sow sparingly to avoid having to thin out too much.
- If you do need to thin out your carrots, do it later in the evening when the flies are less likely to smell the carrots.

CATERPILLARS

Caterpillars can be a major problem, because of the extensive damage they can cause, sometimes completely stripping the leaves from a plant. They are particularly fond of the leaves of cabbages, cauliflowers and Brussels sprouts. Getting rid of caterpillars can be a time cosnuming business involving trial and error, but there are several remedies you can attempt.

Natural control of caterpillars

- Pick them off by hand.
- Crush the eggs as soon as you see them.
- Place sticky bands around the base of the plants.
- Encourage beneficial predators, such as frogs, lizards and wasps.

CELERY FLY

The white grubs of the celery fly burrow into the leaves of the celery plant, especially in spring. When the fly has struck, you will notice white or brown patches on the leaves. If the attack comes early in the season and in large numbers, foliage can be seriously damaged, resulting in stunted growth.

Natural control of celery fly

- Control by removing and destroying all infested leaves as soon as you notice the first sign of damage.

CHLOROSIS

Chlorosis is a yellowing of leaf tissue due to a lack of chlorophyll. It can be caused by a number of conditions, such as lack of iron and manganese, nitrogen or magnesium. It can also be caused by waterlogging, low temperatures or contamination by weedkillers. It generally affects plants that love acid, so making sure they get enough acid is a sure way of keeping this under control.

Natural control of chlorosis

- Top up the soil with an acidic mulch or fertilizer.

CODLING MOTHS

The caterpillars of the codling moth tunnel into the fruit of pear and apple trees, making them inedible by the time the fruit ripens. If you look closely you will be able to see small exit holes on the fruit.

Natural control of coddling moths

- Suspend pheromone traps from the trees in late spring to mid-summer to catch the male moths; this will prevent the fertilization of eggs.
- Collect any dropped fruit each week, because caterpillars leave dropped fruit very quickly.
- Remove any fruit with holes when you

harvest, making sure you either bury these apples, or put them in a black plastic bag in the sun for at least a month. Composting does not destroy the caterpillars.

CLUBROOT

Clubroot causes a deformity in the roots of cabbages, cauliflowers, sprouts, swedes and turnips. It is caused by spores that can remain dormant in the soil for 20 years while waiting for a suitable host. The roots become stubby and swollen and can develop wet rot. This fungus prefers moist, warm, acid soils.

Natural control of clubroot

- Sowing crops in the autumn when the soil is cooler helps to reduce the risk.
- Raising your own plants from seed should avoid the chance of bringing the disease in on transplants.
- Put lime in the soil and adhere to a strict crop rotation.
- Remove and burn all affected crops.

CUCUMBER MOSAIC

Cucumber mosaic virus can affect all members of the cucurbit family, so don't be fooled by the name. The cucumber mosaic virus overwinters in perennial weeds and can be transmitted to your vegetables via aphids. Leaves of affected plants will turn a mottled, mosaic-patterned yellow and the plant will quickly lose condition. Flowering is reduced or ceases entirely.

Natural control of cucumber mosaic

- There is no cure for cucumber mosaic, so affected plants need to be destroyed.
- The risk of infection can be reduced by keeping aphids under control and destroying them as soon as they are spotted.
- Keep up a strict weeding regime.

CUTWORMS

Cutworms are the caterpillars of certain types of moth that live in the soil. They come out at night and feed on the base of plants, especially lettuces. They will also attack beets, cabbage, broccoli, kale and cauliflower. You will notice that the stems are partially eaten, causing the plant to wilt and grow poorly. They are stout, soft-bodied and grey to dull brown in colour.

Natural control of cutworms

- Before planting remove weeds and plant debris to starve any developing larvae.
- Lay fleece to prevent the moths laying eggs in the soil.
- Birds, ants and parasitic wasps prey on cutworms, so encourage them into your garden.
- Wait until dark and hand pick the caterpillars, dropping them into a bucket of salty water.
- Place cardboard collars around the stems of the plants.
- After harvest pick up all garden debris and turn the soil over to disturb overwintering larvae.

DAMPING OFF

Damping off can affect all seedlings and is caused by a fungus in the water or soil. It is a common problem encountered by gardeners and it can quickly kill a whole tray of seedlings as it spreads rapidly.

Natural control of damping off

- Hygiene at all stages of propagation is essential. Make sure all seed trays and compost are sterilized.
- Do not sow seeds too densely and keep the trays well ventilated.
- Do not overwater and use mains water.

DOWNY MILDEW

Downy mildew is a fungal disease that loves cool, moist conditions. It appears as dirty-white, fluffy spots on the underside of leaves. It especially affects young plants of the brassica family in spring. It can also attack lettuces, courgettes and onions, but can be prevented by choosing disease-resistant varieties.

Natural control of downy mildew

- Give plenty of space when planting to allow a good air flow.
- Remove all debris that might carry spores and also weeds that can act as hosts.
- Try not to wet foliage when watering.

- Practice good crop rotation.

EARWIGS

Earwigs can be a pest because they eat their way through leaves, flowers and vegetables. They are easy to recognize from the pincers at the ends of their abdomens. They are primarily nocturnal, feeding at night, and are attracted by light. They like to seek shelter under organic matter and prefer dark, damp areas, so it is advisable to clear away any debris.

Natural control of earwigs

- Fill flowerpots with straw and place upside down on the top of canes among the affected crop. The earwigs will crawl into the flowerpots during the day and you can empty them in the evening.
- Encourage natural predators, such as toads and birds.
- Make a trap out of rolled-up newspaper or an old piece of hosepipe. Place it near the plants and empty the contents into a bucket of water daily.

EELWORMS

Some strains of eelworms are actually beneficial, but some types may can cause serious damage to vegetables such as onions, peas, beans, carrots, potatoes, cucumber, lettuces, tomatoes and other salad crops. Strawberries are especially susceptible. They are mainly a problem in late summer or early autumn. The foliage of affected plants turns yellow at first then dark brown, as the nematodes move along the larger veins of the leaves. Eelworms spread more rapidly when the foliage stays wet, so times of prolonged rain or heavy dew are particularly dangerous. When watering try to wet only the roots rather than the foliage.

Natural control of eelworms
- Choose disease-resistant strains wherever possible and practice strict crop rotation.
- Remove and burn any badly affected plants.

FLEA BEETLES
The flea beetle is a tiny black insect which, like its namesake, jumps when disturbed. The beetles emerge in April and May after winter hibernation. They eat all types of brassicas, leaving holes in them. Seedlings are particularly vulnerable to attack. Protect them by waiting until they are a reasonable size before planting them out.

Natural control of flea beetles
- Use the beetles' habit of jumping to your advantage. Coat a piece of cardboard with a sticky substance, leaving one edge of card clean. Brush the clean edge over the top of your plants and as the beetles hop into the air they will stick to the card.
- Plant a highly favoured crop such as radish or daikon close to the main crop. This should attract the beetle away from your main crop, then the trap crop can be harvested and destroyed.

FUSARIUM
Fusarium is a fungal disease that attacks lawns and many types of vegetable. It attacks the roots, turning them black and eventually killing the plant. The early signs are black areas on the stems and leaves, which are often coated with a pinky-coloured fungus.

Natural control of fusarium
- At the first sign of the disease dig up all the affected plants and burn to avoid the spread of the disease.
- Dig up the soil in the immediate area, as this will harbour spores.
- Do not put any affected plants on the compost heap.
- Clean all garden tools thoroughly.
- Try to buy disease-resistant varieties of vegetables.

HALO BLIGHT
Halo blight can affect dwarf French and runner beans. This disease starts as small water-soaked marks on leaves, which gradually turn dark brown. Each spot is surrounded by a bright yellow 'halo', hence the name. Halo blight loves wet weather and looks for any injury on the plant. It is spread by seed and water splash, and favours temperatures in the low to mid 70s.

Natural control of halo blight
- Try to plant disease-free seed.
- Practice strict crop rotation.
- Remove and burn any affected plants.

- Clean any contaminated tools.
- Avoid working with the plants when they are wet, as the bacteria are easily transmitted in droplets of water.

HONEY FUNGUS

Most woody plants are susceptible to honey fungus, as are strawberry, rhubarb and globe artichokes. It is a fungus that primarily exists on dead plant material. It can also become a parasite and feed off living plant and tree roots. Plants affected by honey fungus will not grow very well, are generally discoloured and the fruit is small. You might notice white to cream-coloured growths in the soil at the base of the plant. These fungal growths can have a distinctive, strong mushroom smell.

Natural control of honey fungus

- Dig out and burn all affected plants.
- Try to remove as much of the root system as possible, as this is where the disease is most easily transmitted to other plants.
- In mild cases, remove the top 90 cm of soil and replace with infection-free soil.
- Choose strains that are disease-resistant.
- Keep plants as healthy as possible by regular mulching and feeding.

LEATHERJACKETS

Leatherjackets are the larval stage of the crane fly or 'daddy-long-legs'. They feed on the roots of grass, but will also attack potatoes, strawberries, cabbages and lettuces. Affected plants will turn yellow, wilt and eventually die.

Natural control of leatherjackets

- Cover the ground with black plastic overnight; the leatherjackets will rise to the surface into the moist space. At dawn they can be gathered and put out for the bird – starlings love them.

MEALYBUGS

Mealybugs mainly attack plants that are grown in greenhouses. They are small, oval, sap-sucking insects that can grow up to 4 mm in length. If you look at them closely they resemble a tiny woodlouse that can be either grey or pinkish in colour. The body is covered with a layer of protective wax and when seen in large numbers can resemble small pieces of sticky cotton wool that can be accompanied by sooty mould. It is not easy to get rid of mealybugs, but persistence will pay off in the end.

Natural control of mealybugs

- Discard and burn badly infected plants.
- Leaving plants outdoors over winter is a good way of destroying colonies.
- Scrape or brush off as many insects as you can, or cut out badly affected shoots.
- Use a fatty, acid, soap-based spray and spray fortnightly until no more adults are seen.
- Introducing a natural predator, such as ladybirds, can drastically reduce infestations.

MOSAIC VIRUS

Although similar in appearance to cucumber mosaic virus, this disease is spread by seeds and not aphids. It affects potatoes, beans and lettuces.

Natural control of mosaic virus

- Dig up and burn all affected plants.
- Make sure you wash your hands and tools after handling any affected plant.
- Always use a different site for planting replacement crops.
- Try to buy disease-resistant plants where possible.

ONION FLIES

Onion flies attack all of the onion family, eating the roots and tunnelling into the bulb itself.

Natural control of onion flies

- Prevention is the best cure for onion flies. Practice strict crop rotation and protect emerging seedlings with fleece.
- Make sure you remove and destroy any onions as soon as you see signs of onion-fly maggots, so they do not have a chance to enter the soil and pupate.
- Make sure you collect all onions at the end of the harvest. Do not leave any in the soil for the maggots to thrive on.

PEACH LEAF CURL

This is a fungal infection that affects peaches and nectarines. The fungus overwinters in the bark of the trees and waits for young leaves to appear before attacking. The leaves will change in colour to a dark red, appear deformed and curled, then fall off. The diseased leaves will be replaced by new unaffected ones, but repeated attacks can eventually kill the tree.

Natural control of peach leaf curl

- Remove all the fruit from the tree as they will not fully develop after an attack of peach leaf curl.
- Do not overwater, but do not allow the ground to become completely dry.
- Apply a nitrogen-rich fertilizer to the base of the tree and water in.

POWDERY MILDEW

Powdery mildew can attack a wide range of vegetables and appears as a dry, powdery bloom on the upper sides of the leaves. It loves hot, dry conditions. The fungal spores travel through the air or by water that is splashed on to plants, particularly on those growing in very dry soils.

Natural control of powdery mildew

- During the dry weather make sure you keep plants well watered.
- Remove all affected plants and burn.
- Mulch soil to retain moisture.

RED SPIDER MITES

Red spider mites tend to attack plants grown in greenhouses. They are tiny, wingless insects that love hot, dry, dusty conditions. The first signs of red spider mites are either small spider webs high up on the plant, or a white speckling on the upper surface of the leaves. They can ruin foliage and reduce yields of vegetables, fruit and salad crops.

Natural control of red spider mites

- Spider mites hate damp conditions, so spray your plants regularly with water. Damp down your greenhouse on warm days to prevent the mites from becoming established.
- You can introduce the natural predator, the mite *Phytoseiulus persimilis*.
- Disinfect the greenhouse during the winter months.

ROOT ROT

Root rot is a fungal infection that affects beans, peas, tomatoes, cucumber and vegetables that are grown in containers. It causes the rootsof the plants to turn black, making the leaves wilt and will eventually destroy the plant entirely. Early symptoms that are visible above ground include the yellowing of leaves and a lack of new growth. Badly affected plants will often have a restricted root growth that enables the plant to be moved about easily within the soil.

Natural control of root rot

- Prevent the disease by practicing good crop rotation.
- Use sterilized compost and mains water.
- If you are growing on wet clay or clay loam soils, incorporate peat or bark mulch before planting and do not plant too deep.
- Pull up and burn any diseased plants.
- Dig up and remove any soil that contained the diseased plants as this will harbour the spores of root rot.

RUST

There are several different types of fungal rust that can affect many varieties of fruit, also garlic, onions, leeks and broad beans. Rust appears as raised, round, rust-coloured areas on the underside of leaves. The infection can spread quickly through the air via spores and wet, warm leaves are ideal for spreading this disease.

Natural control of rust

- Hygiene is paramount – make sure you remove all affected plants and burn. Ensure all fallen leaves are removed from the top soil before they start to decompose.
- Adhere to a strict crop rotation.
- Allow plenty of space between plants and tree limbs for air to circulate.

SAWFLY

Sawfly come in various species that attack different plants, for example, apples, plums and gooseberries. The larvae can often be seen on the edges of leaves and will curl up in an 'S' shape when disturbed. They bore into developing fruits and leave a distinctive scar on the outside. Telltale signs include transparent patches on leaves where the young larvae have been feeding.

Natural control of sawfly

- There is no sure cure for sawfly, so it is best to inspect bushes and trees every week from April/May onwards and remove the larvae by hand.
- Position any susceptible plants in an open position where birds can feed on the larvae.
- Choose disease-resistant strains.

SCAB

Scab is an infection on the skin of potatoes, identified by raised scab-like patches that grow and eventually split the surface. The flesh of the potato is not usually affected, and the scab usually comes away with the skin after cooking. The cause is a bacterium called *Streptomyces scabies*, which is usually present in sandy soil with a high lime content. Low moisture levels during hot, dry summers, can also promote its development. Areas where brassicas have recently been grown are more prone to scab disease. As scab damage is only cosmetic, it is not considered to be a serious problem.

Natural control of scab

- Do not add lime to ground where potatoes are to be grown.

- Add a few handfuls of grass clippings when planting, as this increases the acidity as it decomposes.
- Buy disease-resistant strains such as King Edward.

SCALE INSECTS

These insects are brown and can best be described as a miniature turtle. They are about 3 mm long and are usually found along the centre vein on the underside of a leaf where they suck the sap. They excrete a sticky substance that attracts other insects, such as ants and wasps. They attack apples, bay, cherries, citrus, figs, peaches and vines. Although they do not cause major damage, they can slow down the growth of the plant and also cause sooty mould similar to aphids.

Natural control of scale insects

- It is possible to remove the scales if the plant is not too big by using your fingernail or a toothbrush to scrape them off the leaves. You will probably have to repeat it a few times, but you should be successful if you persist.
- Spray larger trees with a cold tar wash in winter.

SCLEROTINIA

Sclerotinia is a white mould that affects vegetables such as artichokes, celery, carrots and parsnips. As the mould takes hold the affected vegetable will turn brown and slimey as they start to rot.

Natural control of sclerotinia

- Avoid planting susceptible crops in poorly drained soils.
- Weed constantly between rows.
- Avoid planting too densely.
- Choose resistant strains and stick to a strict rotation schedule.
- Remove and burn any affected plants.

SILVER LEAF DISEASE

This is a serious disease that attacks cherries, peaches and plums in particular. The disease is spread by spores that enter any wood that is slightly damaged and can be identified by silver marks that appear on the leaves.

Natural control of silver leaf disease

- Keep under control by pruning off all affected areas, including approximately 30 cm of any healthy surrounding wood. Burn immediately.
- Prevent by pruning in the summer and coating the wounds with a protective paint.

SLUGS AND SNAILS

Slugs and snails are the gardener's worst nightmare. They can rapidly munch their way through foliage, leaving large holes behind them and their tell-tale trails of slime. They tend to remain hidden during daytime, especially in dry conditions, doing most of their damage at night when conditions are cooler and more moist. They will delight in humid, rainy spells.

Natural control of slugs and snails

- Using a torch collect them after dark and drop them into a bucket of salty water.
- Bury jam jars full of beer into the soil up to their necks. The slugs and snails are attracted by the smell and fall in and drown.
- Encourage natural predators, such as frogs, hedgehogs, thrushes and shrews.
- Water the soil with the biological control nematodes.
- It is not advisable to use slug pellets as these can be eaten by birds and the chemical can be recycled back into the food chain.

THRIPS

Thrips are minute flies that lay their eggs mainly on greenhouse plants. They thrive in moist, warm conditions but are so small that you may have a problem identifying them without the aid of a magnifying glass. They feed on plants, very often on the new growth at the tips, leaving a distinctive speckled appearance on the leaves. They particularly love beans, onions and squashes, and are also attracted to bright pink and blue flowers.

Natural control of thrips

- Place some pink or blue sticky traps

around any susceptible plants and inspect regularly.

- Strict sanitation in both the greenhouse and garden can help control thrips, as they love to hide in the nooks and crannies of weeds. Deny them any safe havens by keeping your garden weed-free.
- If you have experienced thrips, dispose of any affected plants and allow a fallow period of one summer before planting in the same area.
- Beneficial insects, such as ladybirds, can help to keep thrips under control.

VERTICILLIUM WILT

Verticillium wilt is another fungal infection that affects many vegetables. The fungus produces a slime that clogs the veins which transport water to the plant. The first sign of the disease is brown markings on the stems and roots; as the disease progresses the leaves start to wilt and turn yellow or brown. Verticillium wilt often starts with wilting at the hottest part of the day with a slight recovery at night.

Natural control of verticillium

- Use a three- to four-year crop rotation. As there are many potential hosts, use corn and grains in the rotation as they are non-hosts.
- Practice strict weed control, as many weeds are hosts of this disease.
- Clean all garden tools thoroughly, paying special attention to secateurs and toppers.
- Dig up and destroy any affected plants.

Remove the soil in the immediate area, as it will host spores.

VIOLET ROOT ROT

This fungal disease is very similar to root rot (see page 149). It will attack asparagus, beetroot, carrots and parsnips and causes their leaves to turn yellow and wilt. The roots of the plants will be coated with a violet-coloured fungus. It loves sandy or peat soils.

Natural control of violet root rot

- Practice good crop rotation management.
- Remove all affected plants and the soil around them and destroy.
- Do not put any affected plants on the compost heap, as this will encourage new spores.

WHITE BLISTER

This fungus attacks brassicas, salsify and scorzonera. It is identified by a white, chalky, blister-like lesion, usually on the underside of the leaf. It also has a sunken yellowish area just above the blister. Wallflowers can be hosts for this fungus and, like most fungal infections, it loves damp conditions.

Natural control of white blister

- Remove all affected plants immediately and burn.
- Avoid overcrowding – ensure that you leave plenty of room for air to circulate between plants.

- When watering, water directly into the soil not on the plant.
- Do not grow alternative host plants in close proximity.

WHITEFLY

These are related to the aphids and like these relatives leave sooty mould on plants. They usually only attack plants inside a greenhouse, but if you live in warmer areas they can be quite destructive – whitefly are insatiable. They have a tendency to shred away new growth and can also spread other harmful diseases.

Natural control of whitefly

- Hang up sticky strips inside the greenhouse and make sure you keep the floor very clean.
- If you spot whitefly in the early stages you can introduce a parasitic wasp (*Encarsia formosa*), which lays its eggs inside the larvae of the whitefly at any time between mid-spring and mid-autumn.

- Ladybirds, lacewings and hoverflies are your best ally against whitefly, so encourage them into your allotment.

WIREWORMS

Wireworms are the larvae of the click beetle, which spend four years in the ground before pupating. They have shiny, yellow-orange bodies and feed on plant roots and bases of root crops. They make tunnels about 3 mm in diameter that can later be invaded by slugs.

Natural control of wireworms

- Lift root crops as soon as possible.
- Crush any wireworms that are visible.
- Cultivate the soil to expose them to birds.
- Traps can be made using chunks of potato buried in the ground. To make them easy to remove attach the chunks to skewers. Hopefully the wireworms will attack your trap which can then be pulled up and destroyed.
- For a biological control, use the nematode *Heterorhabditis megadis*.

GLOSSARY

Acidic With a pH balance below 7.

Alkaline With a pH balance above 7.

Abaxial A surface facing away from the axis to which it is attached.

Annual A plant that completes its life cycle in one year.

Annulus Tissue that forms a circle.

Anther The pollen-bearing part of the stamen.

Apex The tip end.

Apical Pertaining to the apex.

Aquatic A plant that can live in water.

Attenuate Tapered to a slender tip.

Axil The upper angle between the leaf base and stem.

Balanced fertilizer A fertilizer that contains the three main plant nutrients – nitrogen, phosphorus and potassium.

Bare root A transplant that has been lifted from the open soil rather than a container.

Basal Pertaining to the base of the plant.

Beneficial insects Insects that pollinate plants or prey on parasitic pests.

Beneficial nematodes Nematodes that prey on certain garden pests; or ones that help break down organic matter in the soil or compost heaps.

Biennial A plant that needs two years to complete its life cycle.

Biological control Using a naturally occurring organism to control a pest or disease.

Blanching Growing a crop, such as chicory, in the dark to prevent bitterness and to achieve pale, tender shoots. To lightly cook before freezing.

Bloom A whitish powder that covers the surface.

Bolting Premature flowering of a vegetable.

Bract A reduced leaf.

Bractlet A secondary bract.

Branchlet A division of a branch.

Brassica A member of the cabbage family.

Canker A dead spot on a plant caused by a fungus or bacterium.

Cap A hard crust that forms on the surface of the soil.

Catch crop A fast-growing crop that can be used between two longer-growing crops.

Clamp A storage method for vegetables, which involves covering the roots with straw and soil.

Cloche A small, movable plant cover.

Compost The decomposed remains of plants and garden waste. A proprietary growing medium for plants.

Compound fertilizer A fertilizer with more than one plant nutrient.

Corm A swollen, underground stem that resembles a bulb.

Cotyledon A seed leaf of an embryo plant.

Cover crop A crop that is grown to stop weeds and erosion of the soil.

Crown Where the roots and stem meet in certain perennial plants, such as rhubarb and asparagus.

Cut-and-come-again A method of harvesting by cutting off the plant above the central growing point so that it will continue to grow.

Cuttings Sections of plants that are removed and induced to sprout new growth.

Damping off A fungal disease that infects germinating seeds and seedlings.

Deficiency A lack of essential nutrients.

Dibber A tool for making planting holes in soil.

Divisions Sections of perennials formed by dividing in more than part.

Drip hose Part of an irrigation system that has small holes or openings.

Dormant Alive but not actively growing.

Draw hoe A tool for making drills in the soil for sowing seeds, or drawing up soil round plants.

Earthing up Pulling soil up around the base of plants to stabilize the root system, or to protect the plant from light to improve quality.

F1 hybrid The first generation of plants resulting from a cross between two known varieties.

Foliar feeding Applying a fertilizer that is used by the leaves of a plant as opposed to its roots.

Forcing Placing plants in the dark so that the resulting growth is pale and tender. Used for plants such as rhubarb and chicory.

Frame A transparent glass or plastic cover used for plant protection.

Friable Soil that is crumbly and worked to a fine, even texture.

Fungicide A substance used to kill fungal diseases.

Green manure Plants that are grown to cover the ground and then dug in to improve fertility of the soil.

Growbag Commercial sacks of compost in which vegetables can be grown directly.

Hand-picking Removing garden pests by hand.

Harden off Getting plants accustomed to colder conditions.

Herbicide A substance used to kill plant growth.

Horticultural fleece A lightweight synthetic fabric that allows sunlight, air and moisture to penetrate, but provides protection against frosts and pests.

Humus Decomposed organic matter.

Insecticidal soap A commercial mixture of fatty acids that can be diluted with water and sprayed on plants to kill insect pests.

Insecticide A chemical substance used to kill insect pests.

Intensive planting Making the most of limited space by planting crops close together.

Larva(e) Immature stage of an insect.

Leaf mould Decomposed leaves that are used as a compost.

Legumes Plants that belong to the pea and bean family Facaceae.

Loam Fertile soil consisting of a mixture of sand, clay, silt and organic matter.

Main crop A crop that is produced through the main part of the growing season.

Micro-organism A living organism that can only be seen through a microscope.

Mulch A layer of organic or inorganic matter placed on the soil to keep in moisture and to protect it from cold, heat or wind. Also used to suppress weeds.

Nematode Microscopic, thread-like soil-dwelling animals that can be both parasitic and beneficial.

Nitrogen-fixing The ability to convert atmospheric nitrogen into a form useful to plants.

NPK An abbreviation for nitrogen, phosphorus and potassium.

Open-pollinated Plants that have been pollinated by their own variety and not a hybrid.

Organic Deriving from anything that was once alive. A method or science thought to do minimal ecological damage.

Organic matter Soil additives and improvers of organic origin, such as compost, leaf mould or farmyard manure.

Overwinter A method of keeping tender plants through the winter.

Pan A hard area below the soil's surface through which roots cannot penetrate.

Perennial A plant that survives from year to year.

pH The measure of acidity or alkalinity in soil.

Photosynthesis The process by which plants make sugars from sunlight.

Plant out To transplant young plants that have been raised under cover or indoors.

Plug plants Commercially available seedlings that have been grown in individual soil blocks that are ready for planting out.

Pollination The vital fertilization of female parts of a flower by male pollen.

Pot up To plant rooted cuttings or seedlings in individual pots.

Plumule The tip of the shoot as it emerges from the seed.

Potager A formal, decorative vegetable garden, usually on a small scale.

Pricking out Transplanting seedlings to a larger area to give them room to develop.

Propagator Covered trays used to raise seeds or cuttings in controlled conditions.

Radicle The tip of the root as it emerges from a newly growing seed.

Respiration The process by which plants break down sugars for energy.

Rhizome An underground stem that resembles a root.

Rose A plastic or metal head fitted to a watering can to allow the water to come out in a spray.

Rotation Moving groups of crops to a new position in the vegetable garden each year; this avoids excessive soil depletion, and a buildup of pests.

Rosette A cluster of leaves that sprout from a central point and radiate in all directions.

Self-sow To grow from seeds that were naturally distributed in the garden from plants already growing there.

Side-dress To apply fertilizer in a band to the soil surface next to growing crops.

Slow-release fertilizer A fertilizer that can release its nutrients slowly into the soil.

Soil-less compost A growing compost that contains no loam.

Stale seedbed A technique used to reduce the number of weeds in a bed.

Stolon A creeping underground stem that produces new roots and shoots.

Subsoil The infertile layer of soil below the topsoil.

Successional sowing Growing crops in separate sowings about seven to 10 days apart.

Taproot A long, deeply penetrating root.

Tender A plant that is unable to withstand cold weather or frost.

Thinning The process of removing seedlings in a newly germinated row to provide enough space to grow.

Thrips Parasitic insects that feed on plants.

Tilth The condition of a well-worked soil that has been reduced to a friable texture.

Topsoil The fertile top layer of soil.

Trace elements Vital plant nutrients that are only required in small quantities – iron, magnesium, copper and boron are examples.

Transpiration The process by which water is absorbed by the roots, passes through the plant and evaporates through the leaves.

Tuber An underground plant storage organ, such as a potato.

Variety A term used by horticulturists to describe a cultivated variety resulting from controlled breeding techniques or selection.

INDEX